.99

Managing Projects

D0528903

DUCHY-STOKE CLIMSLAND

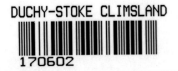

170602

Related titles in the series

Managing Projects

David Nickson

Suzy Siddons

MADE SIMPLE
BOOKS

Made Simple
An imprint of Butterworth-Heinemann
Linacre House, Jordan Hill, Oxford OX2 8DP
A division of Reed Educational and Professional Publishing Ltd

ℛ A member of the Reed Elsevier plc group

OXFORD   BOSTON   JOHANNESBURG
MELBOURNE   NEW DELHI   SINGAPORE

First published 1997

© David Nickson and Suzy Siddons 1997

All rights reserved. No part of this publication may be reproduced in
any material form (including photocopying or storing in any medium by
electronic means and whether or not transiently or incidentally to some
other use of this publication) without the written permission of the
copyright holder except in accordance with the provisions of the Copyright,
Designs and Patents Act 1988 or under the terms of a licence issued by the
Copyright Licensing Agency Ltd, 90 Tottenham Court Road, London,
England W1P 9HE. Applications for the copyright holder's written
permission to reproduce any part of this publication should be addressed
to the publishers

British Library Cataloguing in Publication Data
Nickson, David
    Managing projects
    1.   Industrial project management
    I.   Title II.   Siddons, Suzy, 1942–
    658.4'04

ISBN 0 7506 3471 5

Typeset by Avocet Typeset, Brill, Aylesbury, Bucks
Printed and bound by Martins the Printers, Berwick-upon-Tweed

Contents

Foreword

Crisis management as a management style is well known to us all. It is exciting, easy and immensely satisfying, particularly when a successful reactive response to a major project problem is immediately complimented and seen as an enhancement of the manager's reputation.

Unfortunately, the overall effect of reactive crisis management on the project is likely to be delays, poor resource utilization, low quality work and, significantly, an escalation in cost. In my experience repeated use of this approach leads to lost orders, poor reputation and reduced profitability.

The proven alternative is to proactively manage projects, big or small, using the full range of available project management skills and techniques. It is the only way to guarantee success, and I am therefore delighted to be asked to write a foreword for a book that deals with the critical issue of timely project delivery.

Much has been said and written on this subject and the challenge for David Nickson and Suzy Siddons is to present project management as a vehicle for business success rather than just another topic of conversation. This they have achieved by using their widely differing management skills and experience. This is aptly illustrated in Figure 2.1, which puts all the interrelated project management functions into sharp focus and leads the reader into the well presented detail.

I have known David and Suzy for a number of years and I have had the pleasure of working successfully with them in the project management environment, particularly in the IT market place. Their management approach has always been highly practical with an emphasis on creativity and planning, and it is a perceived management reluctance to move away from the destructive reactive approach that prompted the preparation of this book. It is a serious presentation into which much thought has been put and I am of no doubt that they have put together a narrative that clearly illustrates the way forward – a book that should be read and applied if business success is an objective.

BILL CREASEY OBE, CEng, FIMechE

Formerly a senior logistics and engineering manager in the Royal Air Force, achieving the rank of Air Commodore, Bill Creasey has held senior management appointments in the private sector since 1991. He is currently responsible for the system maintenance line of business within Siemens Nixdorf, the IT arm of the Siemens Corporation

1 Introduction

Make no little plans. They have no magic to stir men's blood. Make big plans: aim high in hope and work. D.H. Burnham

Managing Projects covers a wide range of topics, including project definition, project planning, contingency planning, risk assessment, implementation and delivery, project management tools, project teams, dealing with problems and winding up a completed project.

In order to manage projects well you have to possess a wide range of skills, and the goal of this book is to help provide you with the basis for acquiring them.

Managing Projects has been designed to meet the needs of two groups of readers:

- people in business who wish to improve their team and project management skills to allow them to expand their career horizons;
- those who are studying for a business qualification, including GNVQ, A level, college and first year university students.

To deal with these different audiences the book has been structured so that it can either be used as a textbook in conjunction with a course of lectures and related tutorials, as material for the self taught student, or as course notes/support for a training course.

To do this the book has been built around a core chapter, Chapter 2, 'The project management process'. This covers the basic model of the project life cycle and the theory that relates to it and should be read before any of those that follow it. It introduces the key theme that, although projects are linear in structure with a beginning, middle and end, they are iterative in nature as they take place in a changing world. The reminder of the book is split between what you need to do and the skills and tools you need to do it.

Chapters 3 to 6 cover the activities that need to take place over the life time of a project with examples and exercises that are based on practical experience. Of these Chapters 3, 4 and 6 relate to the project life cycle and Chapter 5 covers the key topic of risk management. These are the 'what to do' chapters.

Chapter 7 provides a brief overview of the types of project management tools that are in common usage and suggests how the reader can decide which are appropriate to the job in hand – a 'how to' chapter.

Chapters 8 to 11 concentrate on the skills and human factors that are required in order to shepherd a project satisfactorily through the life cycle. Particular attention is given to what to do when things go wrong. These are also 'how to' chapters and Chapter 11 is the final 'what to' chapter.

Chapter 12 deals with bringing a project to a close and ensuring that everything has been completed and that no threads are left hanging free.

A Glossary, Bibliography and Sample answers to the exercises given in Chapters 2 to 12 are provided at the end of the book together with the Index.

Given that the reader has completed Chapter 2, and is familiar with the concepts that are presented within it, then any of the other chapters can be dealt with in any order that is convenient. This supports its use either as a linear study course, or to meet specific requirements as needed by the student.

So as to make the book easy to read for those who wish to dip into individual chapters a large number of examples and discussion points have been provided based on real life project situations.

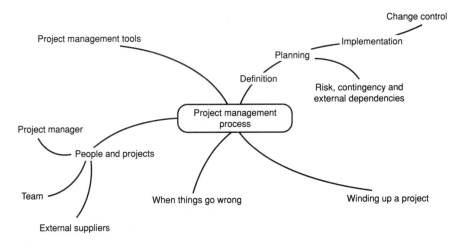

Figure 1.1 Mind map of *Managing Projects*

Figure 1.1 shows that the core chapter of the book is 'The project management process' (Chapter 2) from which five main areas relating to managing projects have been derived: people and projects; project life cycle; project management tools; when things go wrong; and winding up a project.

The purpose of this chapter is to allow you to find your way round the book and have a good grasp of what subject matter is covered. Finally, the authors want to reassure the reader that they have put as high a value on readability and enjoyment as they have on content – and hope that it is, above all, as much fun as you can decently expect to get in a text book!

The project management process

Any military project will take twice as long as planned, cost twice twice as much and produce only half what is wanted. Attrib. Cyrus Vance when US Under Secretary of Defence

2.1 Introduction

This chapter is the core of the book. Once this one has been read, and understood, then the remaining chapters can be taken individually as it suits the reader or the training course being undertaken. It covers what a project is, why projects need managing, the project life cycle, and what the principle areas of concern are when running a project.

2.2 What is a project?

A one-off finite piece of work with fixed start and end points and a clear objective. The difference between projects and ongoing work is that projects have a defined beginning and end, as opposed to being part of a continuing activity. For example building a house is a project, living in one is not. Similarly developing a new accounting system is a project, using it to do the monthly payroll isn't. It should be noted that the one-off qualifier is important. A repetitive procedure for producing something, for example building up an engine from a kit of parts on an assembly line, is not a project.

Discuss the difference between projects and other work/activities. Draw on your own experience to find your own examples.

2.3 Why do projects need to be managed?

In any job that is undertaken there is an element of planning, organizing and prioritizing. These are management activities. For example, consider a project to organize a concert. It will be necessary to plan when it is to take place, what time it should start and finish, where it should take place, what publicity will be needed, deadlines for printing tickets and programmes, etc. Individually all these are relatively simple tasks, but they all have to happen in the right sequence and require the co-ordination of a number of people and organizations. Furthermore there would be constraints on how much can be spent on the hire of the hall given the maximum price per ticket and the number of people who could be expected to attend.

In addition the person responsible for managing the project is responsible for ensuring that the project meets the objectives set for it. In our example the project manager is responsible for ensuring that the concert takes place at the required time and place and that the event takes place within the agreed financial limits.

Most importantly of all, projects need to be managed because they exist in a changing world. It is true for all projects whether they be business, social, public or private sector that their environments will change with time. The structure of a project may be linear – it has a beginning, middle and end. However, because of the changing environment that they take place in the route is by no means a straight line. Projects are linear in structure but iterative in nature. This is a major reason for needing a project manager.

Consider doing the laundry for a family. Define the management activities that are involved. For example, separating whites from coloureds, low temperature from high temperature washes, which clothes are needed first, are there any cost savings from washing non-urgent items overnight to benefit from off-peak electricity?

For small projects these activities may be done on a part time basis by members of the team – or for very small projects, as a team of one. However, once projects get beyond a certain size then this management activity becomes so time consuming that it justifies dedicated effort from someone. This person is the project manager. In large and very large projects it may be necessary to have several people running sub-projects within the framework of the projects as a whole.

2.4 How is a project to be managed?

Having established that projects cannot be expected to run themselves, how should it be done? There is no textbook answer to this; there are as many answers as there are project managers. However, nearly all these different approaches have one thing in common, they hang the management of the project on a life cycle. Many different methodologies exist for describing project life cycles. The one adopted here owes no particular allegiance to any methodology and is a generic one which should be relatively easy to map onto other more specific life cycles. The circular graphical representation has to be adopted to underline the iterative nature of a project's evolution from beginning to end.

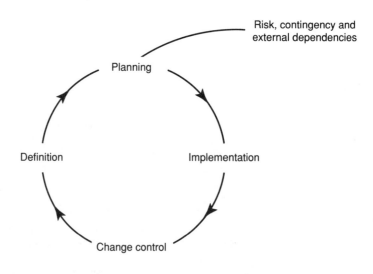

Figure 2.1 Project management process

2.4.1 Project life cycle

This simple model is based on three project stages: definition, planning and implementation. Although it will be covered in more detail both later in this chapter and elsewhere in the book, it should be noted that this does not mean that once a project has been defined then it moves inexorably to its conclusion. Projects are liable to change as they progress and it is likely that the cycle of definition, planning and implementation will be revisited many times before the work is actually completed. This is where theory meets up with real life. The underlying philosophy of this book is that projects have a wider business context and take place within a changing world. A paradoxical consequence of this is that although we define projects as having a linear structure, their evolution is cyclical.

2.4.2 Definition (Stage 1)

This is the starting point for all projects. It is the stage where the project definition is made by the client and the feasibility of the whole project is discussed and examined. It may well be discovered at this stage that the project is not possible – perhaps the time scales are impossible, the budget is ridiculous or the resources are not available, in this case the project should be re-defined or abandoned.

If the definition stage is omitted there will be grave consequences – the project will certainly veer off course, in both time scales and costing.

The first definition that is needed is the statement from the client (the person or people who commission the project, whether internally within the company or externally from a customer). This should cover the basic requirements for the project – time scales, budget and quality standards.

The project objectives (next part of the definition stage) are then drawn up from the project statement. These objectives should be rigorously tested. We suggest using the SMART test. Are the objectives **simple**? Are they **measurable** – how will you know when you have achieved them? Are they **achievable** (has anyone done anything like this before)? Are they **realistic** (in terms of company wide objectives and company resources)? And finally, what is the **time scale**?

Then follows the project management discussion phase where the impact of taking on this project on overall company objectives is discussed, and at a later stage, a meeting with the client to further define the project statement.

The impact of the project on the organization bears careful scrutiny along the lines of the old medical story 'The operation was a complete success but the patient died'. For example a computer manufacturer set up a maintenance contract with a customer – this was done on a project based to run for a fixed time. The pricing was based upon an assumption that there would be a certain number of fault calls per day. In reality the number of calls was many times that used to calculate the price. The project manager was able to run the project perfectly well, however the impact of the additional calls meant that instead of making money for the company the loss was so large that it could have threatened the viability of the whole organization. The project manager identified this and attempts at re-negotiation were made. Successful implementation of this project on its own would have been a disaster for the company as a whole.

Similarly it is vital to check with the people for whom the project is being produced – the 'customer' – that what is being produced is what they are expecting. We know of one family who thought themselves rather clever to go on holiday leaving the decorators to paint all the downstairs rooms in their house. The idea was that all the disruption would take place while they were away enjoying themselves. This all worked very well until they came back and found that all the work had been beautifully done, everything was tidy, but instead of getting cream walls with dark brown skirting boards they had brown walls with cream skirting boards. At least the decorators had the excuse that there was no-one available to check with, but it was a classic example of an efficiently executed project which produced a product that was not at all what the customer wanted.

Next comes the work breakdown structure where the project is broken down into related chunks – this is not a detailed breakdown, simply a look at what areas need to be organized. The idea is to produce a hierarchical breakdown as shown in Figure 2.2 (see also Chapter 3 for details).

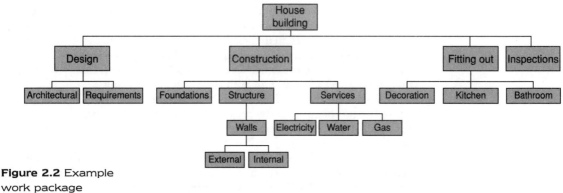

Figure 2.2 Example work package breakdown structure

This is followed by the final phase of the definition stage – resource requirements. Here the staffing, materials and plant requirements are worked out. The goal is to establish roughly what mix of skills and in roughly in what quantities, will be required to deliver the project.

2.4.3 Planning (Stage 2)

The planning stage takes place before any of the actual project work commences. Here the project is planned in detail and specific people are appointed to perform the tasks that are needed (responsibility assignment). The project is broken down into detailed tasks and time scales (projected planning), and it is here that the project team may use a variety of tools to help them. Several of these tools will be discussed in Chapter 7.

Next, potential problems are analysed and contingency plans made (arguably one of the most important phases of the project management cycle). Just as potential problems should be analysed, so should potential opportunities. Projects can be used for many useful business activities – setting standards, training staff, looking for future business, liaising with key suppliers, and forging bonds with existing customers, to name but a few.

The final part of the planning cycle is the resource manager schedule where the team is briefed on all aspects of the project (even if they are not involved in all of them), and specified tasks and responsibilities are assigned. The team briefing is usually followed by discussions and input from the team before individual briefings take place.

2.4.4 Implementation (Stage 3)

As mentioned in Section 2.4.1, this stage will undoubtedly require Stages 1 and 2 to be revisited, at least in part, in order to accommodate changes in the objectives for the project and to include changes required to meet with limitations on resources budgets, and technical problems that occur during the implementation of the project.

The implementation stage is where the activities needed to complete the project take place. There are three ongoing activities that occur in the implementation stage: project monitoring and control, project modification and performance analysis.

1 Project management and control

This is the primary task of the project manager. The project leader needs to know at all times how the project is proceeding. Not only in terms of any problems that inevitably arrive but also how the teams are performing. Any slippage of deadlines must be reported as soon as possible since other tasks may be dependent on the completion of these deadlines. Expenditure must be constantly watched, quality standards must be monitored and corrective actions must be taken as soon as the need arises.

2 Project modification

As we mentioned before, there will almost certainly be changes that will need to be made to the project plan – we none of us have a crystal ball that sees into the future of a project. Quite often changes may be made for excellent reasons – work is completed faster or more efficiently than expected, new ways of working may be discovered that improve the quality of the output of the project team or work may even be brought in under budget. However, what is much more likely is that time scales will slip, costs will need to be juggled, the client will make unforseen changes (the closer the outcome of the project is to reality, the more the client re-defines it!), key personnel may be called away, snags and glitches will be discovered, disasters, both natural and man made will occur, lines of communication may become blocked and even the weather may be against you. Be prepared to modify and modify. If this all seems gloomy, one little ray of sunshine might console you – if you have done the potential problem analysis stage thoroughly you may at least know what to expect.

3 Performance analysis

As mentioned in the monitoring and control phase of the implementation stage, performance analysis is necessary not only for the smooth running of the project but also to check that the way you are doing things is the best way. You need to analyse these things:

- your staff on the project;
- any outside contractors involved in the project;
- the processes that are being used in the project.

2.4.5 Project end

After the three ongoing activities in the implementation stage there comes the glorious moment when the project is complete (hopefully under budget, under time and to a higher quality than specified) and the project is then closed down and evaluated.

At the end of a project the team will most often be disbanded, in part if not in whole. Thanks and praise should be given to the high performers and objective criticism too, if necessary. A 'project end get together' is recommended.

It is all too easy to be carried away with the euphoria (or depression) that completion brings and to neglect the closing stages. The formal closedown and evaluation should ideally be carried out within a week of the project ending and while the relevant information is fresh in the project team's minds. If this is impossible (well earned holidays, nervous breakdowns and hangovers often inter-vene) then careful notes should be kept to refresh everyone's memory. The close-down and evaluation must happen – it is just as vital a part of the project as the other phases. A careful closedown evaluation looks to the future and should answer all of the following questions:

- What have we learned from this project in terms of personal, team and company performances?
- What have we learned about the client?
- Is it worth doing business with them again?
- Is there any future business possible from this project?
- Where were we seriously hampered by resource restraints and what should we do about this?
- What new ways of working, communicating, managing have we discovered from this project?
- What has been the overall impact of this project on our company?

2.5 What are the main areas of concern for a project?

As we said, the client is the person who is authorizing or paying for the project, whether that is someone within your company or an external customer. It is the client who will define what he or she wants from the project.

2.5.1 The client

However the client may well not know exactly what is possible, and it is up to the project manager to ensure that the client is made aware of:

- what is possible and what is impossible (you are the expert on this, not the client; if he could do it himself he would not need a project manager;
- the true costs of the project and the true time scales for the project;
- the exact specifications (these may not be the same as the client's original demands);
- the progress of the project (at regular intervals);
- any significant changes that might alter the project statement.

A good working relationship with the client is essential to the smooth running of the project so considerable effort should be made during the project discussion phase to create this.

2.5.2 Time scales

Remember the Cyrus Vance quote at the beginning of the chapter? Even small pro-jects are prone to running over time. There is a simple reason for this. Mechanical planning tools such as PERT, critical path analysis and so on take no account of the foibles of human nature; people are not like machines – they do stop work to have a chat, they do have days when they work more slowly, accidents do happen and we all of us have a tendency to underestimate how long things will take. Contingency planning should take account of this and extra time should be put into the sched-ules to account for it. If the project comes in ahead of time, very few people will grumble. On the same subject, it is important to make sure that there are mile-stones marking each stage of the project, particularly if the project is a long one. The team will need re-motivating regularly if high standards are to be maintained.

2.5.3 Budgets

The same is true of budgets. Rigorous control at all stages should be kept of the costs of each stage of the project. Many project managers see this as a boring chore;

they view themselves as managers not accountants. However, keeping track of the spend and measuring it against what was expected is one of the fundamental ways of establishing that a project is on track. Indeed, most projects have budget as a key objective. This is true for both commercial and non-profit making organizations.

This is by no means straightforward, and there are many different charges that a project can incur in general they come in one of four categories – set-up costs, recurrent costs, material costs and financing costs. What follows is an overview and it will be revisited in more detail in later chapters.

1 Set-up costs

In starting any project there are a number of set-up costs that are incurred as a one-off charge. Typically these might include:

- installing telephone/communication lines;
- office and computer equipment;
- special tools;
- computer software;
- recruitment costs.

2 Recurrent costs

For most projects these tend to be the dominant charges that a project incurs. They include:

- permanent staff costs;
- contract staff costs;
- equipment hire;
- consumables;
- transport and accommodation.

The rate of spend on staff costs tends to start small, build up to a maximum and then decrease as the project runs its course. This is because projects tend to start with a small core team, then build up to a maximum before tailing off as the project is handed over to the customer.

3 Material costs

These are simply the costs of goods and equipment which is bought for later supply to the customer and may include:

- equipment;
- construction materials;
- raw materials;
- sub-assemblies from third parties.

4 Financing costs

These are not immediately obvious to inexperienced project managers. Because you are spending money you are effectively incurring charges equivalent to the interest that the money would have raised if it hadn't been invested in the project. This may seem theoretical, but for large companies which fund expansion by borrowing they can be very real indeed. They can also represent a measure of whether or not the project is worth doing – if you make more money by putting the money in an interest bearing bank account than the project will reap as profit then it bears examination. There may be other reasons why the project should be progressed such as not having staff idle, future business that may depend on the project's success, etc., but disbanding the project should nevertheless be considered.

Related to this are cash flow charges – effectively the interest due on the balance between money spent by the project and money received from the client (see also Section 4.1).

2.5.4 Communication channels

This is probably the most important aspect of successful project management. More projects fail because of poor communication between the project manager and the team, or between the project team itself, not to mention between the project team and outside contractors and the client and the project manager. This is particularly true when long distances are involved and where remote teams are an essential part of the project. It is not only vital to give exact briefings to the team and individuals involved in the project, but to ensure that feedback is constantly given on the progress of the project (not only the formal filing of reports, but 'snagging sessions' where worries and concerns are brought out).

The client needs to be kept firmly in the picture throughout the project – not just contacted when something goes wrong. Everyone involved must know of any significant changes in the project.

The project manager is the hub of the universe when it comes to passing on information to the project team or the client and it is the project manager's prime duty to make sure that he/she is approachable and consistent in the way he/she communicates. One project the authors were involved with came to a complete standstill because the very efficient project manager had set such high and rigid standards (a good thing) in such a dictatorial way (a bad thing) that members of the project team were reluctant to report any failures to him. 'He Who Must Be Obeyed' as we called the project manager, was effectively sidelined while sub-teams within the project team tried to solve their problems for themselves, little realizing that the delays which were happening were seriously affecting other sub-teams. Although in some ways 'He Who Must Be Obeyed' was an excellent project manager (he was brilliant at the definition and planning stages), but his downfall came when his autocratic manner alienated the rest of the team who became expert at finding ways of avoiding communication with him.

2.5.5 Project teams

Project teams are complicated groups. There are two things they have to do: on the one hand they must effectively perform the tasks they are set to do; on the other hand they need to keep the team itself healthy. Teams are more than just a disparate collection of individuals, they have a personality of their own with all the associated strengths and weaknesses of any personality. It is part of the project manager's role to make sure that his or her ream is healthy, and to watch out for difficulties and problems between team members. He/she needs to balance the people within the teams, making sure that team needs for cohesion, leadership, motivation, proportion, energizing, information giving, quality control, contact with the outside world, problem solving, attention to detail, mediation and idea generation are met.

When groups of people come together to work they go through several important stages of development, and the project manager needs to facilitate these stages, ensuring that the team becomes bonded and efficient.

Think about teams that you belonged to in the past (not just at work). Did some teams work faster or slower than others? What 'rituals' and habits did they have? Did every team have the same attitude to the project manager and the client? Which was the best team you ever worked in, and why was it so good?

2.5.6 External factors

No project team exists in a vacuum. There is a multitude of outside influences on the running of a project. How important is the project to the rest of the company? Are the project team's objectives acceptable to the rest of the company? How is the project being funded? Does the project team have to fight for resources? Are these resources shared with other project teams? Do members of this project team also belong to other project teams and does this cause conflict of loyalties? Where are the members of the team based? Are outside contractors involved in the project? Are there any political factors that affect the project? What physical conditions might affect the project?

These external factors must be taken into account at the planning stage. It is all too easy to focus on the internal workings of the project and to make no contingency plans for external factors. The authors know of a project for the relocation of an entire factory from the northern USA to Russia. The new factory location needed 30 days of unbroken sunshine (rain would have made it impossible) to ensure that vital building work was completed before the relocation project started – an example of how dependency on an external factor seriously impacted the success of the project.

2.5.7 Risk management

Finally, in this section on concerns, a brief mention of risk management. All the concerns that have been addressed here, particularly those detailed as external factors in Section 2.5.6, can be looked at as 'risks' to a project. An important factor in running projects successfully is identifying and assessing the importance of anything that might be a risk to the project. These may be trivial risks that affect only a tiny part of the project and can be ignored, or they may be of such a magnitude that should they occur the whole project would fail. At all stages of the project there will be a need for risk management and the reader will find that it is a running theme throughout the project life-cycle in this book. Indeed, Chapter 5 is largely concerned with risk management techniques because it is so vital to the health of a project.

2.6 Summary

Projects are different from routine, everyday work. They have constraints imposed upon them such as time, cost, quality and performance. They are also subject to external influences outside the direct control of the project team. Furthermore, although they have linear structures – beginning, middle, end – the route that they take to get there is likely to involve a number of iterations and evolutions.

To cope with the changing environment that project exist within projects have to be managed. Project management is an activity in its own right that becomes more and more important as the size of the project increases.

Key points for this chapter: the project life cycle model, management activities, project objectives, constraints, external factors and planning and change management.

2.7 Exercises

Why isn't a production line manufacturing process considered to be a project whilst adding a series of identical conservatory kits to a series of different houses might be? Make up further examples from your own experience.

2.7.1 What is a project?

2.7.2 Why do they need managing?

List reasons why you think that projects cannot just be left to themselves. In small projects there may be no full time project manager – is the project still being managed?

2.7.3 Life cycle

Although a project is defined in part by having a start and an end, the life cycle has been represented as being circular. Why is it useful to look at a project this way rather than a simple series of events leading to a conclusion?

Definition

What are the main activities that need to be carried out in order to have completed the definition stage of a project? What information would you expect to have gathered during this stage?

Planning

Imagine that you have agreed to organize a concert for a friend who is just starting out on their solo career. List all the tasks that would need to be done and identify which you could do yourself and which you would have to put out to external suppliers.

Implementing

Why are you likely to re-visit the definition and planning activities during the implementation of the project?

2.7.4 Concerns

List the main causes of concern for a project. In each case give an example of how they can adversely affect a project.

Project management stage 1 – definition

It has long been an axion of mine that the little things are infinitely the most important.
Sir Arthur Conan Doyle

3.1 Introduction

Before you can start a project with any hope of success you must have a definition of what success is! This chapter identifies what needs to be defined before any production work can begin. It also introduces the basic concept of managing risk. It will be noted by the reader that many of the tasks undertaken during the definition stage resurface during the planning and implementation stages. This underlines the reason that the authors have adopted a cyclical representation for the project life cycle rather than a linear one of beginning, middle and end.

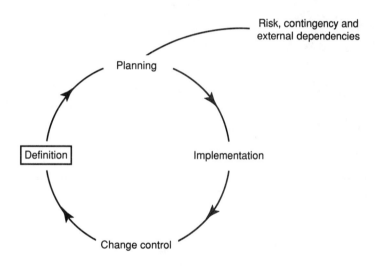

Figure 3.1 Project management process

The goal of the definition stage is to produce agreed goals and objectives for the project and to identify the types of resources required to implement it. In addition the definition stage includes the start of risk analysis and planning and the set-up of the basic project file, etc.

3.2 Project statement

This is the starting point for any project. The project statement must clearly cover the following:

- what the end result will be;
- what the timescales are;
- what the budget is.

The source of project statements is always a client request. This request may be from an internal client (within your own organization) or an external client. In many organizations this statement will come through some type of sales channel.

You should not expect the initial project statement to go into too much detail (that comes later at the planning stage of the project) but it must contain the following elements as a minimum:

- start date;
- end date;
- budget available;
- sign off permissions;
- client contact details;
- terms and conditions;
- legal and safety requirements;
- quality measurements required.

This statement should be carefully read, preferably by all the members of the embryo project team and any areas requiring clarification quickly identified.

For example: design and build a four bedroomed house on an existing plot of land for £80,000 by 12 January that meets planning and building regulations and the terms of the building society loan.

This meets all the criteria for a project and encapsulates the whole project within a single sentence in an unambiguous way.

Consider various projects that you know of and produce project statements for them. Identify any ambiguities in them – how might these be eliminated?

3.3 Goals and objectives

Although the project statement may be clear – design and build a four bedroomed house for £80,000 by 12 January that meets planning and building regulations and the terms of the building society loan – it still remains to define the project's objectives. These define the goals the project must achieve if it is to be considered a success by the client. Simple projects may have only a small number of goals but complex projects will have many goals, some of which may conflict with each other, and it is important to establish this early on.

Determining the goals is the second step in identifying what the client actually wants, and it is essential that these goals are agreed with them before going any further. In addition the goals must be clearly communicated to everyone involved in the project team and to third party suppliers who will be used to supply additional goods or services that may be needed to complete the job.

3.3.1 The SMART test

When defining objectives it is useful to apply the SMART test to establish their validity. SMART stands for:

Simple
Measurable
Achievable
Realistic
Time scale.

For example, 'To have your team paint the town red by Tuesday' is simple, it is measurable (it will have turned red), it isn't achievable using current technology, what's more the citizens might object, you would need immense resources not just a few workers (so it isn't realistic), and the timetable is ludicrous. This is a trivial example, but the same measurement can be applied to any team goal, nothing demotivates people faster than being made to work hard at something that can never be completed. Objectives may be difficult and challenging but they should be achievable and clearly defined.

In the case of building the house, the following objectives have been identified:

- the building must be weatherproof;
- each bedroom must be capable of containing a double bed;
- a central heating system must be included;
- there should be parking for a car;
- the kitchen should have a door to the garden;
- the kitchen should be fitted with compatible units.

Discuss how these meet the SMART test and identify any that may conflict with each other.

3.3.2 Kipling's servants

Once you have checked out the objectives against the SMART test then you must establish how you, in your role as project manager, will implement them. Rudyard Kipling's lines 'I keep six honest serving men (they taught me all I knew); Their names are What and Why and When, and How and Where and Who.' can serve you well here.

For example, the following questions are typical of those you should ask yourself. You will be able to think of more yourself along the same theme:

- **What** resource is need to get the work done? **What** are the external dependencies?
- **Why** do we need to do this? **Why** is it important?
- **When** do we need to start/complete the work? **When** do we need to tell other teams that we have completed it?
- **How** do I motivate the team to do it? **How** do we measure it? **How** will it affect other objectives?
- **Where** do I get the resources? **Where** is the office space for them?
- **Who** is going to help me? **Who** needs to know what actions I am taking? **Who** will benefit from the objective being achieved?

This may seem to be time consuming but, like preparation time spent before cooking a meal, it makes a tremendous difference to the finished result and to the amount of dirty pans (or plans) left over at the end. Faults and potential problems identified before the project has gotten underway are much cheaper to fix than those discovered later on. For example, it is much cheaper to fit air-conditioning to a building when it is being built than it is to add after all the decoration has been completed.

3.4 Project management discussion

This is a valuable communications exercise which can protect projects from the potentially ruinous consequences of assumptions. It is, to some extent, the first step in the risk management process. However, it is a golden opportunity to form the core project team and provide an opportunity to take advantage of creative thoughts before the constraints that come with the day-to-day running of a project descend on the team.

The idea is to get the client representative, probably the salesperson, the project manager and core team members together to thrash out the understanding of what is actually going to be supplied, when and for how much. This is an internal meeting, you may well wish to discuss things that, unless presented in the right light, might undermine the confidence of the client in the successful outcome of the project. Then it is possible to look at all aspects of the project with as few political constraints as is possible.

The format for the meeting is largely a matter for personal preference; some may prefer a formal meeting with an agenda, others a brainstorming approach. Either way minutes should be taken of all key points identified in the meeting.

For larger or more complex projects it may be necessary to split this discussion into separate meetings. For example there may be significant technical detail which is obscure to non-specialists. In this case you might designate a technical team leader to hold a specialist review meeting and then present the outcome of this at a more general meeting.

The following topics should be covered as a minimum:

- resources;
- technical issues;
- costs;
- legal and commercial factors;
- how the project will be handled;
- project viability.

The overall goal for this meeting, or series of meetings, is to get together all the interested parties within your organization and make sure that they all know, and agree with, what is going to be done.

3.5 Deliverables

A logical follow on to the project management discussion is agreement of the deliverables, both directly with the client and internally within the team/organization. This is important as it is the deliverables that enable the project objectives to be met. Additionally the deliverables represent the translation from the project as a collection of concepts into physical reality. The measurable nature of deliverables provide the means to measure the progress, positive or negative, of the project.

Deliverables can be classified in many ways; the authors have chosen to use the terminology defined in the 'PRINCE' methodology preferred by the UK Government (see also Chapter 7). PRINCE is mainly used for computer based projects but the concepts are generally applicable. PRINCE defines deliverables (it calls them products) as management products, quality products and technical products.

- **Management products** include plans, progress reports, organizational charts and other products resulting from management work.
- **Quality products** include error lists, reviews, audits and other products that are a result of quality assurance or control activities.
- **Technical products** these include technical and design information, physical and intellectual products, etc. In other words the deliverables that the project is required to produce in order to meet its goals.

Of these it is the technical products that require a wider definition than the PRINCE one in order to make them generally applicable. If you look at the products as relating to managing, controlling quality and doing the work, then they just about cover any project you can imagine.

For example, in our house building project the following products/deliverables might be identified:

● **Management products**: the project plan, estimates, schedules etc.
● **Quality products**: building inspections, site visits, local government inspection certificates, etc.
● **Technical products**: architects' drawings, building regulations, the foundations, walls, wiring, plumbing, etc.

Think of a number, say three or four, of simple projects that your group might take on. For each of these projects determine what the deliverables might be. Try and group them under the management, quality and technical headings.

3.6 Work breakdown structure

A significant activity required during the definition stage is producing a work breakdown structure. This is used to identify the work that needs to be done down to the level of individual tasks to be performed by one person (or sub-contractor/external project team). The WBS is a hierarchical graphical representation of the work that needs to be done to complete the project. It is important to note that the WBS contains no information on the sequence of events or any dependencies. For example it may tell you that you have to install plumbing in a house and a kitchen, but not that you need the plumbing before you can install the kitchen (see also Chapter 7).

The idea is that you start at the top level of identified activities, for example design, build, test and deliver and then break each of these down through further layers until you reach a level of detail that is appropriate. Normally this would be at the level where one person is doing the task on their own.

The house building project beckons once more.

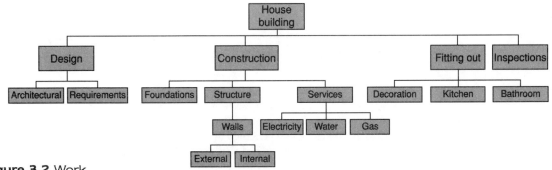

Figure 3.2 Work breakdown structure

As can be seen from Figure 3.2, the structure is a simple hierarchy. At the top level is the house building project itself. This is then broken down into a design, construction, fitting out and inspection sub-projects. The idea is to identify discrete collections of work that are logically related to one another, these may need several people's effort to complete them. This breakdown process is carried on until you end up with tasks that are at the level where only one person is involved, as stated in the introduction to this chapter. This is a key point: in order to manage work effectively it is necessary to have identified who is responsible for it – you can't have two people responsible for one task.

You may come across technical design methodologies that adopt a similar approach to WBS for breaking a project or system down into logical components but representing the information in a different graphical form. For example one method is to draw a box with the system/project inside it and the 'world' outside it. This is then broken down into logical components adopting the same concept as for the more common representation of a WBS. Normally some naming system is used to identify the boxes so that you can follow the flow down easily when presented with a large wodge of paper defining the project structure. For example you might call the top level box 'B', the Design and Construction boxes might then be 'BD' and 'BC', foundations would be BCF, etc. Figure 3.3 shows a simple example of this type of documentation. It is more commonly found as a means of designing computer systems, where it is used to identify the building blocks of the system and allows simple identification of the information that has to pass between them, etc. However, project managers with IT backgrounds have promoted its use in the wider project management arena.

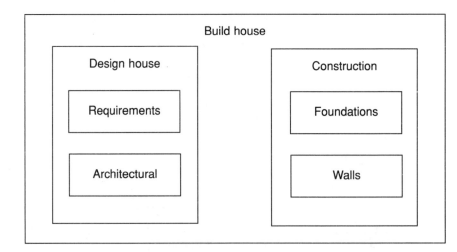

Figure 3.3 Alternative WBS

Whatever method is used to represent the WBS, it is important to be aware that it only provides information about what is to be done, not the sequence in which it is to be done. It is concerned with what, not when. For example, there is nothing in the example WBSs that tells you that the design for the house must be completed before the foundations can be dug.

3.7 Resource requirements

As a result of producing the work breakdown structure it becomes possible to identify the skills required and have a rough idea of how much personnel resources is needed to complete the project.

At this stage the intention is to identify the skills required and get a rough idea of the quantities needed. It is not intended to establish exactly how long the project will take to complete or the exact resource equipment. This will be established during the planning stage (Chapter 4).

For each bottom level activity identified on the WBS, the project manager, aided by the core project team, or as much of it as exists at this stage, determines what skills are required to complete it. For example, to build our house it can be seen that we will need people to produce the architectural plans (an architect!), define the requirement (the people who will live in it), dig the foundations (labourer), build the walls (bricklayer), install the electricity, install the gas and water piping, etc. In many cases the same resource will be needed to do several tasks, but you will end up with a list of skill resources that are needed to complete the project.

Although no detailed estimates can be made at this stage it is worthwhile making a rough attempt at identifying the quantities of each resource type that are needed for the project. The simplest way to do this is to make an estimate on how long each bottom level task will take to complete. If you, as project manager, don't have the knowledge to make these judgements then get estimates from the other members of the project team. Remember that the idea is to get a rough idea of the people who will be needed to implement the project rather than the information needed for an accurate costing/production of a detailed project plan.

The results of the such an exercise could be something like this:

Architect – 5 days
Bricklayer – 30 days
Plumber – 5 days
Electrician – 5 days
Painter – 8 days.

Again, note that the information only gives an idea of total amounts of time needed rather than when they are needed. For example if all the walls had to be completed with a 10 day period then one bricklayer could not provide all 30 days of effort required; three would be needed. This level of detailed information belongs to the planning stage (see Chapter 4).

3.8 Costing

In some organizations much of the definition work will have been completed before the project was 'sold' to the client, in others it may be the case that the first time the project manager becomes involved is when the client has signed the contract! Whichever of these applies to your organization it is still necessary to perform an initial costing exercise at this stage of the project.

During the definition stage the estimate can only be approximate, the main purpose is to provide a confidence check that the project budget is consistent with the amount of work required to deliver it. If there are wild differences then questions need to be asked to determine if the project is really viable.

In essence the costing is simply an extension of the resource estimating process described in Section 3.7. All that is necessary is to multiply the cost of a resource by the amount required to produce the total cost for that resource.

Where the project involves materials (e.g. bricks, etc.) in order to complete it then a similar exercise needs to be carried out for the materials. The example spreadsheet, Figure 3.4, shows a project estimate for the house building project.

House Building Estimate   09.01.97

Resource	Days	Unit cost	Total
Architect	5	£400	£2,000
Builder	25	£120	£3,000
Bricklayer	30	£100	£3,000
Plumber	5	£120	£600
Plasterer	6	£110	£660
Painter	8	£100	£800
Labourer	25	£65	£1,625
Joiner	20	£110	£2,200

		Resources total	£13,885

Materials	Quantity	Unit cost	Total
Land	1	£20,000	£20,000
Bricks	2,000	£0.10	£2,000
Cement	100	£4.30	£430
Sand	100	£2.90	£290
Piping	50	£1.50	£75
Roof tiles	1,400	£0.60	£840

		Material total	£23,635
		Project total	£37,520

Figure 3.4 Example costing

3.9 Risks

During the definition stage a risk assessment exercise should be carried out to establish the risks associated with executing the project. This is covered in considerably more detail in Chapter 5, Risks, contingencies and external dependencies. However, in order to understand the definition process it is important that the reader is at least familiar with the basics during this stage.

3.9.1 Risk identification and assessment

There are many ways of assessing risks to a project. A simple one is to define all risks in terms of two factors:

- Probability – percentage (to nearest 10 per cent or high, medium and low), and
- Impact on project – high, medium and low:
  - high – significant impact, schedule and costs severely affected
  - medium – less serious, impact on only part of the project
  - low – negligible effect.

Essentially the team must agree what level of probability and risk is acceptable to the project.

3.9.2 Risk register

The end product of this is a risk register which details all the risks and the actions/costs associated with them. Figure 3.5 shows a page from a typical risk register.

Risk ID#	Impact (L/M/H)	Probability (L/M/H)	Title/notes
TAX1	Low	Low	Changes to tax rates during project
TAX2	High	Low	Cancellation due to change in tax law
TAX3	Medium	Medium	Late delivery of new computers

Figure 3.5 Example risk register

3.10 The project file   This is a control file, controlled by the project manager, and which contains the documentation that is essential for the project. This file will be of great importance to the project and its importance cannot be overstated. Failure to maintain it can put the future of the project at risk. At definition time this file will largely include planning information, etc., but it should also be designed to contain the documentation relating to the running of the project.

For a running or completed project these would include:

Project plans   Up-to-date and complete copies of all project plans, PERT and Gantt charts, WBSs, etc. It is important that this information is maintained as a high priority. In particular records should be kept of any milestones completed.

Terms of reference   Any terms of reference for the project manager, project staff, etc., should be included to ensure that there is a baseline definition of who is generally responsible for what.

Progress reports   Weekly/monthly/quarterly internal and customer reports provide an audit trail of how project issues have been identified and dealt with and give a record of the evolution of the project.

Forecasts   Associated with progress reports there will be forecasts for time to completion, spend against budget, etc.

Estimates   Resource, material and (derived) cost estimates and most importantly how they were calculated. Again it is important to be able to go back to this information should it become necessary to revalidate the viability of the project.

Minutes of meetings   Inevitably with anything other than a very small project there will be records of meetings held internally and externally. These should be kept in the project file to ensure that they can be referred to in the future and to document any actions that affect the progress/scope of the project.

Change requests   It is important that all requests for change are kept for future reference both to provide an audit trail and to ensure that requests do not get lost!

Risk register   A record of all the risks that were identified for the project, to be updated during the lifetime of the project.

Contracts   Contracts with customers, suppliers, sub-contractors and any letters relating to them are needed both to define the scope of the supply and for use in case of dispute, etc.

Organization charts	Charts covering the project team, the parent organization and supplier/customer organizations wherever possible are useful for determining who to contact and who reports to whom.
Project specifications	Requirements documents/specifications, technical specifications, etc. Further information that defines the detail scope of the project.
Acceptance documentation	As the project progresses there will be some formal documentation referring to the acceptance of project deliverables by the customer(s). These should be kept, particularly where they are related to payments, etc.

Typically the project file will be in the form of a lever-arch or similar large loose leaf binder. The information should be filed in reverse date order, i.e. the newest information in any section is kept at the front of the file.

Of course it may not be possible to keep all the relevant information in a single file. This may be because of the sheer volume of documentation involved – the requirement specifications for large computer systems may run to several volumes in their own right. Or it may be for administrative or quality control reasons – for example it may be desirable to have all change control information kept in a separate file, similarly documentation relating to risks may require its own file.

It is the responsibility of the project manager to ensure that this file is always kept up to date and that members of the project team are aware of its contents and where to look for information that they may need in order to perform their functions within the project. If in doubt a rule of thumb should be that if the project manager was run over then the contents of this file should give a successor all the information needed to take over.

3.11 Summary

Although it seems obvious it is surprising how many projects get underway without any agreed definition of what is to be delivered. These unfortunate endeavours are often impossible to finish to anyone's satisfaction because there is no definition of what the completed project is. As with many occupations the more thorough the preparation the greater the likelihood of a successful outcome. Identifying and agreeing the project goals and objectives inside and outside the project team, identifying and recording risks to the project, determining the skills and organization needed to complete the work, and defining the WBS provide the foundation upon which to build the project.

At the end of the definition stage the project manager should have established the following:

- Project statement
- Identified goals and objectives
- Defined project deliverables
- Project file
- Risk register
- Cost estimate
- Work breakdown structure
- Resource requirements.

3.12 Exercises

Note: These exercises may be linked together to form a case study. Alternatively you might use a real project you are involved in as the basis for similar questions.

3.12.1 Project definition

Imagine that you are the project manager for a project to design and build a prototype portable conference centre. Your team would include structural designers, consultants who know what customers would want from such a centre, architects, transport consultants, interior designers, electricians, plumbers, etc.

Produce a project statement for this project. How would you assess the validity of this statement?

3.12.2 Goals and objectives

Starting with the (or a) project statement identify as many goals and objectives for the project as you can. Use the SMART test to determine the validity of the goals and objectives. Revise these accordingly so that you end up with achievable ones. Do the revised goals fulfil the requirements of the project statement? If they do not what actions might you take?

3.12.3 Deliverables

Define the deliverables for the portable conference centre. These deliverables should include both what is required to produce the prototype itself, what might be needed to support going from a prototype to a production unit and what might be needed to demonstrate the usefulness of the prototype to potential buyers.

Why is it important to agree deliverables with the client? Is it necessary for all the deliverables to be agreed with the client? Who else might you need to agree the deliverables with?

3.12.4 Work breakdown structure

Analyse the project for the portable conference centre and produce a WBS that takes account of the project deliverables and goals. Take this WBS down to the level where one box represents work that will only be carried out by one person. Why is it important to do this?

3.12.5 Resources

For the WBS produced for Question 3.12.4 (or similar) identify the types of resource that would be required to deliver the project. Why can you only make an approximate estimate of the quantity of resource (staff and material) at this stage?

3.12.6 Costing

Using the WBS that was produced for Question 3.12.4 (or similar) allocate the packages to the types of resource identified. make up daily cost rates for these resources (or use real ones if you have them).

3.12.7 Risks

Conduct a risk identification exercise for the prototype portable conference centre. Based on these risks do you consider the project would be worthwhile continuing with? How did you go about making this assessment?

3.12.8 Project management discussion

Why is a project management discussion useful? If you are working in a group, carry out such a discussion for either a project you are involved in or the case study in these exercises.

3.12.9 The project file

What would you expect to have in a project file at the end of the definition stage of the project? What additional information might you plan to include at a later date as the project progresses? If you have completed the other exercises for this chapter, do you have the makings of a project file?

4   Project management stage 2 – planning

Adventure is the result of poor planning. Colonel Blatchford Snell

4.1 Introduction

This chapter covers the production of the initial project plan, what activities are involved in producing it, how the project can be organized, and what needs to be planned for. A key point is that the initial plan is merely a starting point – plans must be continuously revisited and adapted to reflect the reality of working in a changing world.

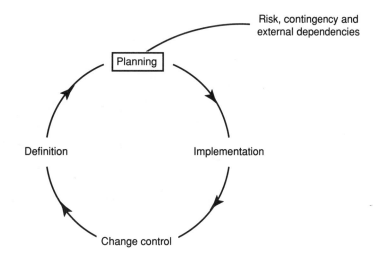

Figure 4.1 Project management process

From the work done in the definition stage the project manager will have:

- established the project statement;
- identified the goals and objectives;
- defined the project deliverables;
- set up the project file;
- set up the risk register;
- produced an initial cost estimate;
- produced a work breakdown structure; and
- defined the resource requirement.

These are the necessary precursors for the planning stage; without this information it is not practical to continue and the definition stage cannot be considered to be complete. This information will have been recorded in the embryo project file set up during the definition stage.

The goal of the planning stage is to expand upon this information to produce a detailed project plan which identifies the resources needed to deliver the project, the time scales involved, the costs, and to make sure that the plan is effectively communicated to all those involved.

4.2 The project plan

There are a wide range of methods and tools available for planning projects and Chapter 7 deals with some of the more common ones in overview. For the purposes of this chapter, where we are concerned more with what needs to be done than how it should be done, examples will be based on a simple bar chart approach (see Section 7.2) which details who does what and when.

One of the purposes of the planning stage is to take the goals and objectives of the project and the WBS (work breakdown structure) and use them as the basis of a project plan. The essential features of the plan are that it identifies who does what and when and in what order.

4.2.1 Resources

During the definition phase the resources required to implement the project were identified in general terms. Now that this has been refined to the level of single task/person, with the addition of time information it is possible to identify the detailed resource requirement in terms of type and number of staff required.

For example time constraints applied to the house building project of Chapter 3 could result in the 'build the walls' activity being split up as shown in Figure 4.2.

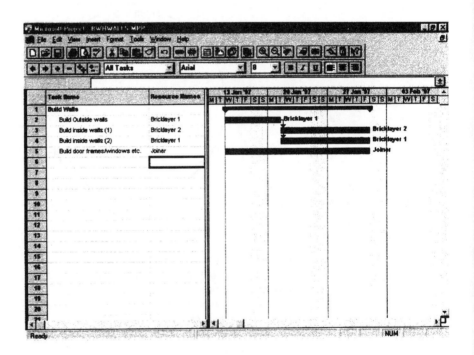

Figure 4.2 Resource allocation

Here the limited time available means that two bricklayers will be needed full time for part of the activity, together with a joiner if the house is to be completed on time. The resource plan shows when these people are needed and the project manager has to either get these people from his/her own organization or an external supplier if the time scale is to be met.

Inevitably, competition for any resources within an organization will lead to negotiations and this is a key skill for a project manager. Chapter 8 provides an introduction to negotiation techniques and how they can be improved. Without the correct resources the project cannot be completed as required. Again, if this is the case the project manager will need to re-negotiate the parameters of the project accordingly.

The other aspect of resource definition is knowing what materials, equipment, transport, logistics, office space and tools, etc., are needed and by when. All the same constraints will apply to obtaining this resource as for the staffing resource. The project manager will need to both negotiate for and facilitate the supply of all resources needed to ensure that the project can be completed as specified.

For example, in the case of a project to move staff from one office to another the items that need to be considered might include packing materials and cases, trolleys and lifting equipment, vehicle hire, temporary storage of the equipment overnight in a warehouse, relocation of telephone and computer equipment, provision of power and data cabling at the new site, etc. All of these would need to be planned for in the same way as the staff resources to pack, move, unpack, de-install, re-install, etc.

4.2.2 Roles and responsibilities

One of the most important things that needs to be determined at the planning stage is who does what – otherwise known as roles and responsibilities. In Phase 1 – definition – a WBS and the resource requirements were identified. In the planning phase this needs to be translated into a detailed resource plan where staff are allocated to specific tasks.

The project plan has told us what type of technical/physical/intellectual skilled resources are needed, and when, to complete the project. This is not the end of the story; once the project team members have been identified then the teams have to be put together and managed in the best way possible to deliver the goods. At this point the project manager needs to look at the personal skills – team leadership, communications, etc. – that the team members have and take these into account when allocating people to roles. For example, the best computer programmer available to a project might not have the leadership and communication skills needed to be a technical team leader. The skills needed by the project manager to take this into account are covered in Chapters 8 and 9.

It is important that once roles and responsibilities are established that the individuals concerned, and the team, are made aware of what these are. For the individual this should include some formal (i.e. written) terms of reference detailing what they are to do, who they report to, who reports to them and what they are expected to deliver. For the team it comes down to briefings, organization and whatever else is deemed necessary to make sure everyone is at least aware of who does what as far as it affects their ability to perform their project role.

4.2.3 Dependencies

A dependency is defined as the link between two activities, one of which must be completed before the other can be started.

Dependencies dictate the flow of the project. Quite simply where one thing must be completed before another one starts then you have a dependency. These exist both within the project and between the project and the outside world (see Chapter 10 on dealing with third parties).

Even something as simple as making a cup of tea is riddled with dependencies. You have to fill the kettle before you can boil the water. You have to put the teabag in the cup before you pour the boiling water over it, etc. On the Gantt chart in Figure 4.3, the dependencies have been shown by the arrows linking tasks that must be completed in a particular sequence. Although the kettle must be filled before the water can be boiled there is nothing to stop you putting the teabag in the cup whilst the kettle boils – there is no dependency between the two activities.

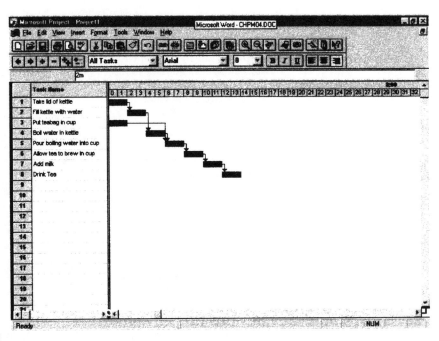

Figure 4.3 Dependencies

Perhaps a more realistic example, though still fairly obvious, is that you have to build the foundations before you build the walls which will support the roof of a house. Of course there may be more than one activity that has to be completed before another starts – someone else (a third party) would have to supply the bricks!

Determining your project dependencies

When producing a project plan you will need to look at all the activities that were identified in the WBS and determine which ones are dependent on others. This is where the hierarchical organization of the work to be done, as identified in the WBS, comes in useful. By having the multi-level organization you can simplify dependencies by keeping them within the same level. For example, you might have a simple top level flow that went Design – Manufacture – Test – Deliver with a simple follow-on dependency. Within each of these you will find that individual activities may be dependent on the delivery of 'products' from other parts of the project or from external suppliers and sub-contractors. However, you would not need to have a dependency from every low-level manufacturing activity to the individual design tasks unless there were individual reasons to do so.

Why might you wish to have dependencies between low-level tasks in different high-level stages of a project?

**Summary of
dependencies**

As stated, dependencies define the sequence in which events occur during the life of a project. Some of these events will be dependent on factors outside the project team working environment – these are known as external dependencies. A simple example of an external dependency is that a project to build a house cannot start until someone agrees to pay for it. Similarly where materials are required there is an external dependency on the supplier of the materials. An example of an internal dependency might be that the painter cannot start painting a wall until after the plasterer has finished plastering the raw brickwork (and allowed time for it to dry out).

4.3 Milestones

A common feature of many project plans are milestones. These are simply identifiable points in a project's life which allow you to demonstrate progress. Whilst they may be quite low level it is more usual for them to be associated with significant events. Typical milestones within a project include award of contract, completion of design, completion of a significant deliverable, delivery of equipment to the customer's premises, acceptance of the project, expiry of a warranty period, etc.

These milestones might be for internal use within the project team or might be agreed with the client as being external milestones against which progress is reported.

One of the uses of milestones is to trigger payment. For example, you might agree a milestone with a client that allows for payment on the completion of the technical design. Where this is done it is essential to make sure that the definition of the milestone is both clearly stated and understood by all concerned – you should agree the deliverables that relate to the milestone in question so that its completion is clearly demonstrable.

Consider a number of projects which you are involved with, or any of the examples given in this book, and determine both internal and external milestones that might be defined.

4.4 Financial

For all intents and purposes all projects have budgetary constraints, though some government defence projects might seem to be exceptions. Indeed the traditional way of rating a project manager's track record is against the criteria on time and **within budget.** Consequently, financial matters rate high on the agenda for most project managers.

During the definition phase a rough cost was determined based on the resources that were to be used. In the planning stage it is possible and convenient to refine this cost by specifying the rate for each resource.

How the charge for resources are calculated within a large organization can be quite complex. For example, how are overheads apportioned between staff working on a project to cover the costs of the office space, phones, parking, etc.? From the point of view of the project manager this tends to be invisible. Typically all staff that are permanently employed by an organization will have a daily 'cost' rate that is charged to the project for time spent working on it. External contractors will have hourly, daily or weekly rates which are paid for in the same way as materials from third parties. In other words the project manager should have an identified 'cost' that is charged for all materials and staff resources.

This means that the project manager can calculate a cost for the project by taking the resource plan and using the appropriate daily/hourly rates as a multiplication factor. This is effectively the same type of calculation that was made at the definition stage – cost for resource multiplied by how much. However it is based on a more accurate picture of the resource required, for example taking into account the limitations of resources/materials available and other constraints. In addition, because the costs are broken down into greater detail it is possible to look at the profile of the spend over time and against particular components of the work.

Figure 4.4 shows the project plan to develop a new prototype widget. Four staff are involved – a designer (D1), a machinist (M1), a technical writer (T1) and a project manager (P1). The daily rates are: £150, £90, £100 and £200 respectively. It has been assumed that all materials were supplied free of charge so only staff costs are incurred. The project manager is planned to spend 10 per cent of available working time on this project, the designer works 80 per cent on this project during the design phase and 100 per cent during other phases in which she is involved. Other resources are assumed to be dedicated to the project when working on it.

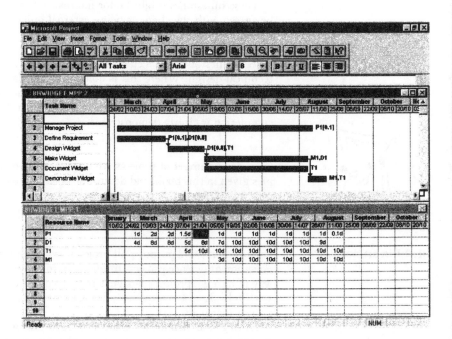

Figure 4.4 Project plan for a widget

Cost for defining the widget:	£3,750	(resource P1 and D1)
Cost for designing the widget:	£4,600	(resource D1 and T1)
Cost for manufacture:	£14,880	(D1 and M1)
Cost for documentation:	£6,200	(T1)
Project management:	£2,320	(resource P1)
Demonstration (T1 and M1):	£2,090	
Cost for whole project:	£33,840	

Monthly cost:

Month	March	April	May	June	July	August
Cost	£3,360	£4,110	£6,600	£7,560	£8,280	£3,930

Cost for each resource type:

P1 (project manager, part time)	£2,920
D1 (designer, mainly full time)	£14,850
T1 (technical writer, full time)	£9,500
M1 (machinist, full time)	£6,570

4.4.1 Cash flow

Following on from this there is usually a need to know what the project's cash flow is. Cash flow is the next step up in sophistication from simply waiting until the end of a project, subtracting what it cost from what was paid by the customer and, hopefully, ending up with break even or better.

Cash flow is defined as 'The difference between money in and out from a business or project measured over a specific time'.

Most commonly cash flow will be measured on a monthly or weekly basis.

Consider the widget prototype. In this case the payments are made as follows – 10 per cent at the start, 30 per cent on completion of the design, and the balance of 60 per cent on delivery. The price for the widget prototype was calculated to give a small profit of £2,000 making a total price of £35,840. Over the six months of the project this would lead to the following cash flow (assuming the project runs exactly to plan).

Month	March	April	May	June	July	August
Money out (cost)	£3,360	£4,110	£6,600	£7,560	£8,280	£3,930
Money in (price)	£3,584	£0	£10,752	£0	£0	£21,504
Cash flow	+ £224	– £4,110	+ £4,152	– £7,560	– £8,280	+ £17,574
Running balance	+ £224	– £3,886	+ £266	– £7,294	– £15,574	+ £2,000

It can be seen that although the project made a profit of £2,000 overall for the 6 months, the project had a negative cash flow in the fourth and fifth months that peaked at £15,574 which would have had to be found by borrowing.

Cash flow charges

Whilst it would be nice if all projects has a neutral, or better, cash flow, sometimes they have periods of negative cash flow. This is usually because the client wants to protect themselves from risk by holding back as much money as possible until the project is completed. Consequently it may well run at a loss for a considerable period. When this is the case it is common to include some additional allowance for the interest that this borrowing implies. This is known as a cash flow charge.

For example if you were to assume that interest was due at 1 per cent per month on money owed then the widget would incur charges in April, June and July of £38.86, £75.60 and £155.74 respectively, a total of £270.20 in all. These would barely be offset at all by the interest that could be obtained from £224 and £266 in March and May (about £5!).

Cash flow in the real world

As a foot note to this subsection on cash flow it is worth noting that the situation is further complicated by the fact that there is a lag between both costs being incurred and prices being charged (as invoices etc.). This brings us into the world of credit control and the accountant, something which is not directly the responsibility of the project manager. However, a good project manager will keep a watching brief on the overall finances from a business perspective. Failure to do so can lead to problems as the project progresses if financial pressures due to poor cash flow or late payments, etc., impact on the smooth relationships between subcontractors, customers and suppliers.

4.4.2 Mark-ups and margins

Although control of costs is the main focus of the project manager the wider business requirements demand that there is a thorough understanding of profit, the return the company makes on its investment in delivering a project to a customer. To this end it is important to note the difference between costs and prices as defined by mark-ups and margins. This is because the price to the customer will be a sale price whereas what the project manager is aware of is costs. If you are unaware how prices are calculated then it will be difficult, if not impossible, to understand how well the project is doing in financial terms and how to negotiate changes in the price to the client for changes to the project deliverables.

Margin is the percentage of the sale *price* that is profit.

If you sell something for £100 at a 20 per cent margin then the cost price would be £80.

Mark-up is the percentage of the *cost* that is added to reach the sale price.

If you sell something that costs £80 with a 25 per cent mark-up then the sale price is £100.

To the casual observer the margin seems to understate the situation when compared to a mark up. This is so. It helps to remember that a margin of 50 per cent means a mark-up of 100 per cent.

When working out if your project is performing well financially you need to know not only the price to the customer but also the margin or mark-up the project is meant to achieve.

Consider a project to deliver a payroll system to a customer for £50,000. The supplier expects this to be delivered with a 25 per cent gross margin. This means that the cost price is expected to be £37,500. You could express this as a mark-up of 33.3 per cent if you prefer. What impact would a £3,750 overspend have on the gross margin?

Answer: 17.5 per cent. So a 10 per cent overspend reduces the profitability by 7.5/25 = 0.3, nearly a third.

In other words what can be viewed as a relatively small overspend can have a significant impact on the return that a company might expect to get on the project. In the example an overspend of 33.3 per cent would mean the project would just break even – not allowing for financing charges.

In addition to this resource cost there are also third party and material costs to be considered.

4.5 Risks

Chapter 5 deals with risks and their assessment in some length and the reader is referred there for detailed information concerning the factors to consider. However, it should be noted that the planning stage is a natural point at which to review the risks that were identified during the definition stage, preferably involving the wider audience now available and taking account of the increased amount of information available to the team. This is part of the ongoing risk management that should continue throughout the project lifetime.

As at the definition stage any risks which might have a severe impact on the project should be carefully reviewed. It is better to abort a project at an early stage when relatively small amounts of time, effort and money have been expended than to carry on regardless spending vastly more money and taking resource away from other potentially worthwhile projects.

This review process should include re-visiting all the originally identified risks and identifying any new ones. Naturally the results of this process will need recording in the risk register and communicating to any interested parties.

4.6 Problem analysis

Just as we had the project discussion sessions associated with the definition phase (see Chapter 3), there is a need to assess and discuss any problems that can be identified during the planning phase. This is a distinct exercise from the risk analysis that was started during definition, and it continues throughout the life of the project. In risk analysis you are looking at threats to the project and assessing their potential impact – effectively looking at things outside the control of the project team. Here the idea is to review the problems that the team can identify within the project itself and look at ways of solving them.

This is very important. Essentially, you must not make the mistake of thinking that after all the work done during definition and producing the plan you have thought of everything and you can sit arms folded waiting for nature to take its course and the project will arrive neatly packaged at the appointed date spot on budget. It won't! You only have to consider all those 'laws' that exist :

Brook's Law: 'Adding manpower to a software project makes it later.'

The old Army saying: 'An order that can be misunderstood will be misunderstood.'

and of course the famous

Murphy's Law: 'If anything can go wrong, it will.'

The philosophy of the problem analysis phase is much the same as for the project discussion except that the work is being considered in greater detail. Although described as problem analysis, the emphasis is on finding solutions and proposing a way forward rather than building up an insurmountable heap of problems first and then despairing of finding a solution afterwards. The aim is to identify the general approach that will be taken to deliver each aspect of the project rather than to complete detailed design work, etc. In larger projects the requirement for prototyping or piloting particular aspects of the project may be identified as being necessary before a detailed commitment can be made.

It is a natural consequence of the problem solving work that new tasks may be identified and existing tasks as specified in the plan may well take longer or, if you're lucky, shorter than originally estimated and this information needs to be collected and fed back into the evolving project plan.

Obviously the larger and more complex the project the more time will need to be spent on the problem analysis. However, even if you are running a very small project you should at least go through each stage and assess what the problems are.

As with the project discussion (Chapter 3) you may well split this problem analysis into specialist groups to look at — for example, specific technical issues. These are then reported back by group leaders at the general project forum.

4.7 Opportunities

Whilst people are focused on the job in hand it is very easy to be oblivious to opportunities that present themselves. The project manager should always be looking for at the project in its overall context — what opportunities exist for future business? Are there skills or other indirect benefits that the team can develop as a result of doing the project that can be used in the future? Can the project be used as the basis for on-the-job training for new/inexperienced staff? Is there an opportunity to apply new technologies? The possibilities exist and it is up to the project manager to make sure that they are capitalized on.

During the project planning stage there exists a one-off situation where everyone is fresh to the project but in possession of the basic facts. Consequently they should not have too many pre-conceived ideas as to what is to happen. Furthermore, people have not yet got settled in to their everyday project life so they still have some time available to take a wider view. This makes this the best time to look outside of the project and establish any opportunities that might exist for capitalizing on the deliverables in a wider arena. 'Spin off' is phrase that is frequently used to describe benefits from or applications of a project outside its original context.

There are many examples of spin off. Perhaps one of the most famous is the non-stick coating for frying pans that was originally developed for the early US NASA space projects. Another was the micro-computer from the Apollo moon explorations which has led to a whole personal computer industry.

These high tech examples are at the high end of spin-off applications. However, at the more mundane level there are often opportunities that can be realized from projects in other areas which may make significant benefits to the sponsoring organization without requiring significant effort from the project team. A trivial example might be that to complete a job some equipment, for example a computer graphics design program, might need to be purchased which would be of use to another part of the company later on, thus getting more value from the package. Similarly if a member of the project team required training in a particular skill it may well be that a market for this skill exists in the wider market place and that person could sell a service to other organizations, thus producing a new revenue stream.

From your own experience think of examples where there were opportunities for spin off from a project you are aware of. Was the opportunity taken? If not, why not? If so, to what effect?

4.8 Task scheduling

In this section we are concerned with the handing over of work to individual members of the project team, not the process of scheduling tasks within a project to meet resource/time constraints, etc. Effectively this a form of delegation (see Chapter 8).

At the planning stage this is where the tasks are initially handed over to the project team. This will be done via a combination of team and individual meetings. The mixture of team and 'one-to-one' meetings will depend on the size of the team, the size of the project, etc. It may be more effective to provide a seminar, with accompanying reference material to cover the general information that applies to the project team and then hold smaller/individual meetings that cover issues that relate only to those people concerned.

However, whatever mix of meetings and seminars is considered, the information that each team member needs is as follows:

Project	An overview of the background to the project, what it is for in general terms and why it being implemented.
Client	An overview of the client, their business/organization and how the project fits into this environment.
Goals and objectives	The principle goals and objectives that have been agreed for the project and their relative importance to the success of the project. Overview of any critical success factors (CSFs) that apply.
Time scales	An introduction to the time scales that apply to the project, when major milestones are expected to occur.
Benefits/importance	Why the project matters to the client and the supplier, what the benefits will be from the successful completion of the project.
WBS	An introduction to the work breakdown structure for the project so that everyone is aware of how the project has been analysed.
Project plan	An overview of the structure and logic of the plan. Identification of the principle internal and external project deliverables and milestones.
Project organization	Who does what. An overview of the organization chart for the project.
Dependencies	Highlight key dependencies, especially those that involve third parties and sub-contractors.
Critical tasks	Identify the activities that are critical to the project's success so that everyone knows which are the important tasks, etc.
Roles and responsibilities	Everyone should be made aware of the general roles and responsibilities that apply to everyone (including third parties) involved in the project. At the very least everyone in the project should know the job titles of all involved. People's detailed tasks will be passed to them directly.
Questions and answers	You should include these at the end of any project briefing session and encourage staff to question anything they are unsure of. In one-to-one sessions you should

encourage interactive questioning as you go along. The project manager is responsible for making sure that everyone knows what is going on and their part in it.

It is important that everyone in a project knows what is going on, why, and who does what, etc. Without this background information the scope for misunderstanding and everyone going off in their own direction independent of project goals is immense. Do not skimp on this part of the planning process.

4.9 The project file

This section is a simple reminder to the manager to update the project file with the new information and plans that have come into being during the planning stage. The file may be used to provide background briefing information to new team members as well as to provide the audit trail/central register for the project. It is possible that the project file may need to be split into different levels of confidentiality – for example some information may be confidential within the team, some may even be confidential to the project manager such as financial details and trade secrets, etc.

4.10 Agreement of plans

It is one thing having detailed plans of how much it is going to cost, when it is going to be finished and what is to be delivered. However, without the agreement of all involved these plans are not worth the paper or magnetic media upon which they are recorded. Ideally all staff should agree that the tasks they have been allocated are reasonable and that they can deliver on time and to budget. As a minimum it is vital that the customer for the project agrees on the big three of time, cost and deliverable.

Ideally the plans should be subject to sign-off by representatives of all involved. In formal project development methodologies (see Chapter 7) this might be a project control board that includes representatives of the client, the sponsoring organization and any third parties, sub-contractors and representatives of the project team. Whatever approach is taken it is essential that plans are agreed and not just made and then ignored.

It is usual for the project plan to be a 'controlled' document. As a minimum this will involve some formal process that has to be completed before it is re-issued to show changes. It may also contain commercially sensitive information and require distribution control.

4.11 Summary

The production of the project plans, and their agreement with all concerned, provides the foundation for a successful project. The plan needs to cover resource, financial, deliverables and time constraints to provide a baseline against which the project can be monitored. The plan also documents the logical flow of the project in terms of sequence of activities and identifies all the external dependencies, etc. It provides the bridge between knowing what is required to make the project a success and the work that has to be done to deliver it.

At the end of the initial planning stage the following additions will have been made to the project information:

- an agreed project plan (including Gantt/PERT charts, etc.);
- resource plan and organization chart;
- risk plan;
- revised and more detailed cost estimate;
- agreed time scale and deliveries;

● agreed change control procedures.

These will all need to be recorded in the project file together with the documents from the definition stage:

● the project statement;
● the identified goals and objectives;
● the defined project deliverables;
● the risk register;
● an initial cost estimate;
● a work breakdown structure;
● the resource requirement.

Although the iterative nature of project planning was covered in Chapters 2 and 3, it is such an important concept that is going to be repeated here. **'The plan is never complete until the project is finished.'**

4.12 Exercises

Note: If you prefer you may continue using the prototype portable conference centre project from Chapter 3 as the basis of these exercises instead of the examples given here.

4.12.1 Project planning

Produce a project plan for building a small business centre. This would require parking, office space, reception and meeting areas, computer and telephone facilities for up to 10 people. Use either a Gantt or PERT chart (see also Chapter 7). Although it is not necessary to cover all the aspects as you would for a real plan, do not over simplify. From the plan identify internal and external dependencies and what resources will be required when. Similarly identify any points on the plan which might make good milestones for either progress monitoring or triggering payment.

4.12.2 Resource

Resource identification

To what level must you break down the work to be done in a project? Why is this important?

Resource limitations

In the example given in Section 4.2.1, the 'build the walls' activity has been broken down to allow more than one bricklayer to work on it to reduce the overall time scale. Given that more bricklayers were made available to the project manager, what limitations might there be on further reductions to the time scale?

4.12.3 Roles and responsibilities

What factors would you consider when assigning roles and responsibilities to members of a project team? Why is it important that these are well defined and what measures would you take to ensure that everyone knows who does what?

4.12.4 Dependencies

You have been made responsible for the catering for a family birthday party at which there will be 30 people. Some are vegetarian, some meat eating. A room has been provided with kitchen facilities in which you can hold the party. The event is in a week's time and you have two people to help you who can shop, cook, set up tables or whatever will be required. You have to serve at least five courses of which three will need to be served hot. Produce a simple project plan for this that covers choosing the menu, determining what raw materials need to be purchased, setting up the room, doing the preparation and cooking, serving the meal, etc. What internal and external dependencies exist within your plan?

4.12.5 Financial

Using the plan for the birthday party as a basis (or making up a new one if you prefer) imagine that you work for a catering company. You have been asked to manage the project and to produce a financial plan. You can assume that it will cost you £30 per person to provide the food and that the staff you use will cost you £5 per hour each and that you must use them in minimum quantities of half a day (4 hours) at a time. Your time costs £100 per day and your minimum charge out period is one day. You may assume that everything else is provided free of charge (FOC).

Calculate what the project will cost to deliver. What price would you charge if the company required you to make a 20 per cent margin? What price would you charge if you were required to operate a 20 per cent mark-up?

The client has negotiated an agreement where they pay for the party one month after it took place. Why might this reduce the overall profit of the job? How might you allow for this?

4.12.6 Risks

Consider a project to build an out-of-town shopping centre. Identify as many sources of risk to the project as possible. For all these risks make an assessment of both how likely they are to occur and how great an impact they might make on the project. Which of these risks would you consider when assessing the ongoing viability of the project? Why would you record all the risks identified, not just some of them?

4.12.7 Project file

At the end of the planning stage what additional information would you expect the project file to include? Who would you expect to have access to the project file, and would you expect there to be restrictions to access to the file?

4.12.8 Opportunities

Why is it important to identify any non-project specific opportunities for the business or organization that is sponsoring the project? Either look at a project you are currently involved in or consider one which involves the design of a system for cataloguing video tapes. What opportunities can you identify? If there is no formal procedure for passing on such ideas within your organization, who would you inform?

4.12.9 Task scheduling

You are the project manager of a team who are to produce a new expenses processing system for a transport/courier company. The team will buy the computers, write the computer software, provide training to the operators and promote the use of the system within the company. Perhaps 20 people are involved all together including technical programming staff, team leaders, trainers, buyers, personnel and accounting staff. How would you go about tasking these different staff? What information would you give to all of them and what would you make person specific? Where teams are involved, what involvement in this would you pass on to the team leader and how would you make sure that everyone involved was correctly tasked?

5 Risk, contingency and external dependencies

Never take anything for granted. Benjamin Disraeli

For those seeking a quiet life as a project manager the answer is to plan for what can go wrong before it happens. The old saying 'If it can go wrong, it will' proves itself true time and time again. This chapter suggests ways of planning and allowing for the unexpected.

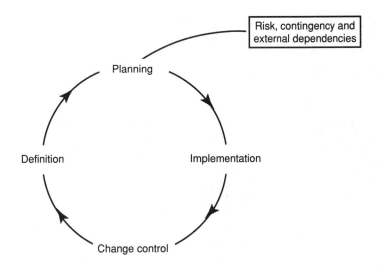

Figure 5.1 Project management process

5.1 Introduction

Life is a continual process of taking risks, either calculated or blind ones. Even making a cup of tea has the risk that you may scald yourself if you knock the teapot over just as you are pouring the boiling water. Of course all risks are not associated with physical danger; you may find that you have run out of tea bags – hardly life threatening but it brings the project to an untimely end pending a trip to the shops. Similarly a lack of milk wouldn't stop you making tea, but it might reduce the quality of the end product from the point of view of the consumer.

This chapter covers three related, overlapping and consequently sometimes confused, topics: risks, contingencies and external dependencies. Indeed, there are good excuses why this confusion takes place as subtle changes in interpretation can turn a risk into a contingency from the point of view of cost estimation. Furthermore, in many ways risks and contingencies can be seen as before-the-event change management exercises. These three have been collected together in this chapter because there is a common thread linking them as threats to the successful completion of any project. Although most of the material relates to risks, it will be found that the same techniques can usefully be applied to contingencies and external dependencies.

The strict definition of these planning activities will vary from one formal methodology and organization to another, but in general the definitions supplied will serve for all practical purposes. It is important that the reader gains a clear understanding of the difference between a risk and a contingency within their organization and can communicate this information to other members of a project team to ensure a common understanding.

Risk planning is increasingly becoming a required activity for those running projects in both the government and private sectors. The larger the project the more likely this is, but even the smallest project can reap considerable benefits from a short time spent analysing and planning for risks. The basic concepts of risk planning and analysis are presented and the reader should be able to produce a risk plan once these have been assimilated.

5.2 Definitions

5.2.1 Risk

An event or situation for which there is no corrective action that can be taken and which can endanger part or all of the project.

Risks are events outside the control of the project team. In some cases it would be possible to have a plan of action which could be brought into play should a risk occur – bringing it into the territory of a contingency (see Section 5.2.2).

In the case of a family house self-building project there are a number examples that spring to mind:

- redundancy could make the project financially impossible;
- changes in planning rules could make the house unsuitable for family needs;
- expansion of a local industrial park could adversely affect property values.

It is important to note that the risks can come in all shapes and sizes from the merely irritating to the catastrophic. The point of identifying all the risks to a project is to enable you to make an informed decision as to whether the potential risks to the project are outweighed by the benefits of completing the project. In addition, time taken in identifying risks can allow you to eliminate many potentially 'unforeseen' problems during the lifetime of the project.

In some cases risks can impact the business case for a project rather than the physical viability of the project itself. For example a take-over of one company by another could result in a change in infrastructure that could remove the need for a project in one or other of the organizations. The project could perfectly well be completed successfully and achieve all its goals, but there is no longer a need for it.

5.2.2 Contingency

An activity or allowance that will have to be made should a specific situation arise.

or alternatively,

A risk for which you have chosen to have an action plan should it occur.

Typically, contingencies are planned to cover events, usually undesirable, that may take place at various stages within the project, requiring additional work to be undertaken. If you like you can think of a contingency as being a special case of a risk, one which you can do something about. Indeed, during the process of risk planning some risks will cross the boundary from risk to contingency as a result of identifying actions to take to minimize the impact of the risk.

For example, our self-build family identified that painting of the exterior wood-work on their house was going to be very weather dependent. As this was one of the jobs they planned to do themselves, it would have to be done during their planned vacation time. This was going to be in October, when the weather could not be guaranteed. Their contingency plan for rain was that they would take any removable items such as doors and opening windows off and paint them in the garage and then employ someone to paint the remainder at a later date when the weather was better. Any remaining time would be spent on interior decoration. They built this potential additional cost of hiring a painter into their contingency budget.

The principle benefit of identifying and costing all the contingencies that apply to a project is that it makes it possible to come up with a realistic cost for delivering the project. Of course, taking into account, and building in a cost for, every possible contingency may well make a project economically unfeasible. A view has to be taken on what can and cannot be covered. The project manager then needs to agree with the customers for the project which events are covered and which are not – see the section on negotiation in Chapter 8.

5.2.3 External dependency

A reliance on a third party outside the direct control of the project to supply a component/service necessary for the completion of the project.

Back with our house building project, an obvious example of an external dependency is a bricklayer not being able to start building a wall until after the builders' merchant has delivered the bricks.

Of course, it can be argued that any external dependency has a risk associated with it and that, therefore, an external dependency is just a sub-category of a risk. However, external dependencies are so often the cause of problems for projects because of the increased difficulty of communicating with a third party that they have been given their own section by the authors to underline the importance of paying significant attention to them. Indeed, such is the importance of dealing effectively with third party suppliers, etc., that an entire chapter has been provided on the subject – Chapter 10.

5.3 Risk

Risk planning and risk analysis are subjects in their own right and there are entire books available on the subject. Indeed, for very large government projects risk analysis and planning can involve whole teams of people on a full time basis. However, a general awareness of how to assess risks and make judgements about them is essential for anyone managing a project, and it is the goal of this section to provide the reader with this awareness. Although restricted in scope by the space available, what is missing is largely the statistical treatment of risks and risk networks, etc., which is irrelevant to 99 per cent of working project managers. Consequently, what remains should serve the reader well enough for the majority of business projects that they are likely to encounter in the early stages of their career.

5.3.1 Benefits of risk management

By identifying potential risks to a project you put the project team in the position of someone who is 'forewarned and therefore forearmed'. By being aware of what the risks are, you will be able to identify warning signs and act quickly to minimize or eliminate their impact. In addition, by identifying the high risk areas to a project it is possible to make a decision early on that a project is too risky to continue and therefore avoid the situation of starting a project that is doomed to failure. It is much cheaper to abandon a project early on than to wait for a disaster after 90 per cent or more of the effort and money has been spent. Also, it is possible to look at changing elements of the project so that risks can be avoided. For example, in the case where a possible change in government due to an election was likely to cause the cancellation of a project you might suggest delaying the start of the work until after the election takes place. Of course, it may not always be possible to take such avoiding action but, if you don't identify the risks you remove the opportunity to do so altogether.

The benefits are thus the increased chance of delivering the project on time and to budget, combined with significantly decreased chance of being ambushed by the unexpected. Not to mention increased peace of mind for the project team.

5.3.2 Sources of risk

There are many sources of risk to a project. However, in practice they can be split into two categories:

- **External risks:** risks affecting the viability of the project from the outside world and business environment.
- **Internal risks:** risks that come from within the project, e.g. the tools used by the project team, technical issues, staff ability, etc.

5.3.3 Risk identification

The starting point for dealing with risks is to identify them. There are two common approaches to this. One is to gather the project team, plus any customer, supplier and sub-contractor representatives who can be persuaded to attend, for a brainstorming meeting. At this meeting everyone is encouraged to state any and every risk they can think of, however unlikely. These are then recorded and an assessment is made as to the likely impact of the risks in terms of probability, cost, time scale and severity.

The other approach is more formal, consisting of a series of interviews with all those identified as having a view on the project – essentially the same people as for the brainstorming exercise. At these interviews the each individual is asked what risks they think exist, how probable they are and what the likely impact would be were they to occur. Figure 5.2 shows an example of a form that could be used to record risks at the interview stage.

In either case it is essential that everyone involved with the project is actively involved in identifying the risks and is made aware of the outcome of any related analysis, particularly where the risks are directly relevant to the work they are doing individually. Risk management can only work if the whole project team is committed to it in theory and in practice.

Risk # *TAX2*	Severity *High* High/Medium/Low	Probability *Low* High/Medium/Low	Date *12 January '97*
Description *Cancellation due to change in Tax Law*			
Interviewer: *David Nickson*		Interviewee: *Suzy Siddons*	

Figure 5.2 Example risk identification form

It is the author's view that for small projects the brainstorming approach is the superior one because duplicate risks are identified more quickly and the meeting provides an opportunity to present risk management in a positive light and to raise the general understanding of the risks to the project as a whole. For larger projects this approach is more difficult to achieve for logistical reasons; it may be too expensive and/or impractical to get all those needed together in a manageable forum. Here it is better to adopt the structured interview method and accept that it will take a little longer to perform the risk analysis.

In both cases it is also necessary to assess the importance of the risks. As this exercise will be taking place during the start-up stages of the project the information that people have available to them will be either speculative or based on experience. Consequently it is not sensible to use an over specific measure of risks such as percentage or even marks out of ten as the implied precision is not justified by the information available. A simple approach is to specify the risk to the project in terms of low, medium and high impact and the probability of a risk happening as low, medium and high.

The following definitions are provided as guidance for the reader. Though, as stated many times in this book, judgement has to be exercised when deciding how serious a risk is.

Low impact: minor or negligible effect on either time scale or cost.

Examples:

- specified paint only available in 1 litre cans not 2.5 litre cans, limited cost change;
- minor change in health and safety regulations requires cables to be run through trunking rather than across floor, minor changes in cabling cost and time to install.

Medium impact: a noticeable but not extreme impact on time scale and/or cost.

Examples:

- fluctuation in exchange rates impacting the price of essential components, cost penalty in proportion to quantity involved;
- change in building regulations could require foundations to be dug to a lower depth, associated time scale and cost impact;
- short-term delay in availability of new products needed for the project, time scale change.

High impact: a significant or catastrophic impact on the project in terms of both time scales and costs.

Examples:

- change of government could result in policy change, entire project could be cancelled;
- serious delay in availability of new technology equipment essential for the project, significant time scale and, possibly, cost increases;
- discovery of geological fault along planned route of road resulting in massive additional work required, major cost increases out of proportion to value of work to the business.

5.3.4 Risk register

The risk register provides a central record of all the risks that have been identified. Figure 5.3 shows an example extract from a risk register. The risk ID# has been used to link the risk to a group of activities.

Risk ID#	Impact (L/M/H)	Probability (L/M/H)	Title/notes
TAX1	Low	High	Changes to tax rates during project
TAX2	High	Low	Cancellation due to change in tax law
TAX3	Medium	Medium	Late delivery of new computers

Figure 5.3 Example of a risk register

This register is not just a one-off document it is a 'live' document. Whenever the project changes (e.g. as a result of change requests, etc.) it is important to revisit the appropriate parts of the risk plan and update the risk register where necessary. See also sections on risk in Chapters 2 and 6.

Consider the case where as a result of a change it has become necessary to delay the start of a particular task by one month. However to do this task a specialist piece of machinery is required which is only available from one local equipment hirer. The equipment has been pre-booked, but there is now a new, or modified risk, that the equipment may no longer be available – it could have been hired out to someone else already and so not be there when needed for the rescheduled work.

5.3.5 Risk analysis

Risk analysis, in essence, is a ranking exercise. The risk register that was created by compiling the results of the risk identification work contains all the risks to the project together with their potential impact on the project and the probability of them happening. As was stated before all probabilities and impacts have been categorized as low, medium and high.

A simple, pragmatic and highly practical analysis method is to use a simple filter on the identified risks – effectively setting a minimum cut-off for the product of risk and probability by saying that if it is unlikely to happen or it doesn't impact the project very much then forget it.

The following two-step process can be used:

- Step 1 – eliminate all low-impact risks regardless of probability;
- Step 2 – eliminate all low-probability, medium-impact risks.

Note: This has been expressed in steps so that at the completion of each stage the risk manager (project manager/team, etc.) can take time to reflect on the ranking that has been given to the risks, in particular when eliminating the low-probability, medium-impact risks.

What remains are the high/medium-impact and medium/high-probability risks. These can now be ranked as follows:

Impact/probability	Ranking
High impact, high probability	Very high – unacceptable
High impact, medium probability	High – potentially unacceptable
Medium impact, high probability	High
Medium impact, medium probability	Medium

Of course the validity of these rankings is dependent on how the risks were scored when the project team, etc. were determining what the risks were. If in doubt revisit any risks that seem as though they might be in the wrong pigeon hole.

As a guideline the following consequences of risks at these rankings are given:

- **Very high – unacceptable.** Any risk which is thus ranked would be expected to endanger the viability, or even the potential ability to complete the project in its business context. You should not expect there to be many, or even any, of these for a viable project.
- **High – potentially unacceptable.** Again these can be expected to seriously endanger the project but are less likely to happen. You should not expect there to be many of these if the project is safe to continue with.
- **High.** These are serious threats to either the time scale or cost of the project. Typically they would be expected to make a major milestone impossible to meet or push a project into a break even or loss making position.
- **Medium.** These are still significant and individually could make a milestone be late or a cost overrun on a specific element of the project. As long as there are not too many of these then the project is still a viable one.

As mentioned in the introduction to this section, the detailed statistical and mathematical modelling aspects of risk analysis are beyond the scope of this book. However, just in case someone is trying to blind you with science it is worthwhile being aware of some techniques that may be encountered.

The first step up in complexity from simply identifying the high/medium-risk, high-probability combinations is to assign actual percentages to probability and an impact rating of 1 to 9. For instance, the chances of a change of government during the lifetime of the project might be given an impact rating of 9, perhaps cancelling the project. The probability might be given as 1 per cent for the lifetime of the project (six months in this case).

This allows a more sophisticated approach to be taken, multiplying ratings with percentage to produce composite risk values. As stated, the authors are dubious of the value of this as there does not seem to be the information available required to back up the implied level of accuracy given by the numbers. However, it does provide the raw information needed for those who wish to make risk models of their projects that follow the same structure as their project plan (see Chapter 7). In this case each low-level task has risks associated with it and these are then built up through the project to produce overall risks for the project as a whole and to identify individual project areas which carry more risks than others. This can be useful as it focuses attention on specific parts of the project which seem to be a greater risk of failure, perhaps planning for back-up resources to cover the problem if necessary, although this is really turning a risk into a contingency.

The risk analysis provides a major input into any go/no-go decision affecting the project's future, both at the start-up time for the project and at any time during the project's lifetime. Risks need to be continuously monitored from the beginning to the end of the project.

The bottom line of the risk analysis is to provide the information needed to decide if the project is a good bet in terms of the likelihood of a good outcome, despite the potential for factors *outside* the control of the project team to disrupt progress.

5.3.6 Financial considerations

When estimating how much a project should cost it is common place to include some allowance for unexpected costs that result from risks, etc. At the crudest level this can just be someone adding on 10 per cent to the total based on the number that comes from the project plan to provide some kind of buffer for when things go wrong. The risk management process described here can be used to provide a slightly more scientific approach to this. By estimating how much additional cost will be incurred for each risk identified and then making an estimate of how likely they are to occur to the nearest 10 or 20 per cent you can then come up with an allowance based on the product of the cost and the probability.

For example, you might decide that it would cost an extra £5000 to meet new planning regulations if they came into force during the construction of a new warehouse. You might have been informed that there was only a small, say 20 per cent, chance of this happening. Taking these two together you could make an allowance of 20 per cent of £5000 = £1000 when calculating your costs for the project.

The adoption of this approach is only useful if the price to be charged for the project is determined after the risk analysis has been completed. The sales cycle of many companies often precludes this, sometimes to their cost!

5.3.7 Risk plans

Now that all the risks have been identified (hopefully) and ranked, it is necessary to produce a plan saying how they are to be dealt with. It is the responsibility of the project manager, or for large projects a separately identified risk manager, to produce a risk plan for the project in hand. The plan is effectively documenting what the risks are and what action you would take if they came about.

To do this it needs to include certain information for every risk to be documented, possibly on a form similar to that shown in Figure 5.4.

Note: low level risks can simply be left as documented in the risk register, though remember that any risk can change in importance/probability during the lifetime of the project.

Risk	Severity High/Medium/Low	Probability High/Medium/Low	Date
Description A brief description of the risk, including the source, what specifically will be the effect on the project if it comes to pass and other relevant information that helps identify the risk. What the probability of the risk happening is (from the risk register etc.).			
Consequence		Action	

Figure 5.4 Risk form

The collected individual risk documents form the risk plan for the project. For a large project it might be useful to include an introductory document which provides a management summary of the risks and provides background information about the project so that a reader can gain a good idea of the major risks to the project without having to wade through a large amount of information relating to relatively unimportant risks.

As with all aspects of project working there needs to be a balance between the amount of effort put into risk management and the benefits that are to be realized. It is perfectly possible to produce a detailed risk plan that identifies all risks down to the lowest level task for the entire project. Indeed, the authors have seen such plans where the risk register included the probabilities of delays in distributing meeting minutes due to photocopier failure! The balance needs to be made between making sure that you have identified all the medium and high probability/impact risks that would endanger the project and having a risk register two feet thick that identifies a vast number of risks that are of no consequence. In other words a judgement has to be made as to where to draw the line between useful work and diminishing returns.

5.4 Contingencies

As defined earlier, contingencies are events that you plan for. If X happens then we will do Y to take it into account is what contingencies come down to. Typically they are associated with the extra resource/time needed, though occasionally a contingency can indicate a reduction in time/resource requirement, though experience has led the authors to believe that this is rare, if not unknown. They differ from risks mainly in that they are largely within the control of the project team and the immediate customers.

For example, when implementing a new computerized engineering scheduling system, the system might be designed to cope with 100 engineers initially. However when the original specification was made it was stated that there might be a requirement to cope with an extra 50 engineers. Therefore there is a need for a contingency plan to cope with this change should it occur. In some ways you can look at contingency planning as change management before the event.

5.4.1 Contingency plans

Contingencies tend to fall out from the project planning process. They are related to things which are going to happen. For each contingency identified within a project there needs to be a contingency plan that identifies what is to be done, by whom and how much it is going to cost. In this aspect it is just the same as any other planned activity. Consequently the contingency plan is simply an extension to the main project plan with the significant difference that it is only activated when a pre-determined set of events have come into being.

For example, consider the following situation. The project is to implement a new stock control system for a small warehouse. A key part of the system is the use of hand held bar code scanners (devices that read the codes made up of black lines on a white background found on most types of packaging). At the time of starting the project it was not possible to determine if these would be supplied by manufacturer A or manufacturer B. Both products would fulfil the function; the decision depends on who is able to supply the required quantity in time for the warehouse to re-open as scheduled. However the device supplied by manufacturer A requires the use of a non-standard computer program to translate the codes into the form used by the stock control system. This software program is provided free of charge by the supplier but would need to be integrated with the rest of the system. The extra work required to do this is small – one day's effort – and the resources would be available from within the project team.

Figure 5.5 shows how this activity fits in with the overall plan. As there would be a significant amount of time within which this one day's effort could be supplied, the activation of the contingency action plan does not represent a threat to the timely completion of the job. However, it does represent a cost to the project of perhaps half a day to administer the work and a charge for this should be allowed for in the project cost.

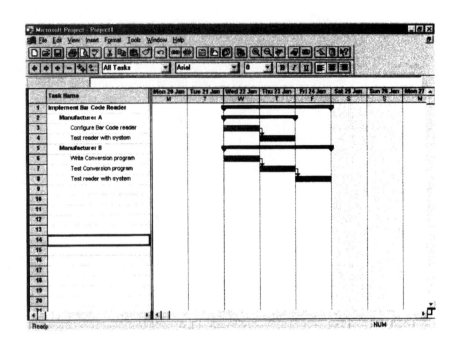

Figure 5.5 Contingency example

5.4.2 Financial

Where additional work has to take place to cover a contingency, this has a price tag associated with it. It is an important part of the project plan to allow for these potential additional costs. Consequently it is necessary to calculate the costs and savings that are associated with a contingency in exactly the same way as is done when calculating the original cost of the project, or as is done when costing changes.

The project is to build a footbridge across a small stream. The initial specification was for a bridge 1 m wide bridging a gap of 6 m with a wooden deck. There is the possibility that, to meet changing safety regulations, it may be necessary to have a deck with a Tarmac surface. In both cases the structure of the bridge would be the same, but the provision of a Tarmac finish would require two additional finishing processes in order to complete the job. Each of these would require the use of specialist equipment and labour in addition to that needed for the basic bridge.

Ideally contingency costs are either built into the total cost for the project or they are specified as being outside the scope of supply but are quoted for as extra cost items to the client. The latter is the fairer approach as the client does not have to pay for something they do not need. Alternatively the same approach can be taken as for a risk – an estimate of how likely a contingency is to happen is made and an allowance made in the costings, and therefore price, accordingly.

5.5 External dependencies

External dependencies have been included in this chapter because, by definition, anything which is dependent on someone or some organization which is outside of your control has an element of risk associated with it. However, because of the special problems associated with dealing with third parties, readers should see also Chapter 10 which deals specifically with the issues involved.

Typically such dependencies occur where a project team is obtaining goods or services from a third party supplier. A kit car manufacturer might build the body and interior fittings themselves but may well buy the engine and running gear in from large-scale manufacturers because the cost of setting up a production line for engines, etc., would be far higher than their volume of business could justify.

The most common problems that a project is likely to encounter arising from third party suppliers in terms of deliverables are associated with timely delivery and changes in costs.

5.5.1 Lead times

It is important to note that there are often lead times associated with the supply of goods and services from the outside world. This also applies to changes to what/when these are required. In other words when considering external dependencies you need to take account of the extra time that will be needed to respond to events.

5.5.2 Associated cost

When examining the dependencies it is important to determine the effect on the project of non-delivery (as with all other risks). For instance if a computer to control the tills in a supermarket is delivered a week later than is intended, then the supermarket cannot open on time. This has the effect of not only having to reschedule the installation, incurring staff wages when the store isn't earning money, but also, most importantly of all, losing a whole week's turnover and profit. The impact on the business could well be out of all proportion to the cost of the computer. Consequently it is essential to assess not only what action would have to be taken to obtain the deliverable but what the knock on cost to the project, and the customer, might be.

5.6 Summary

The key point about risks, contingencies and external dependencies is that they cannot be looked upon as one-off items. It is essential to monitor them throughout the life of the project and review their importance and likely impact. A primary cause of lateness and overspend in projects is the failure to allow for contingencies and to assess risks before the project starts and to identify new ones as the project progresses. In some ways risks and contingencies can be viewed as before-the-event change control exercises – all involve the assessment of the impact on the project in terms of costs and time scales should some event take place. The skills required to handle change can be utilized when dealing with risks and contingencies.

It is also important that project managers keep risks and contingencies in perspective. When looking at risks the idea is to provide a basis for a decision to go ahead/continue with the project and the amount of time spent assessing them should reflect this. Similarly with contingencies the aim is to make provision for those contingencies which are reasonably likely to be needed – it is wasteful to plan for minor contingencies which are unlikely to be required.

Managing risks and allowing for contingencies will not guarantee a quiet life, but it will at least keep the noise level down.

5.7 Exercises

5.7.1 Risks

Identification

Consider a self-build housing project. Make a list of at least 20 things that you think might go wrong and then decide which of them can be planned for as risks, contingencies and dependencies.

Assessment

For the risks that you have identified, rank them according to both priority and probability. Which risks would you discard as being irrelevant?

Management

Why is risk management important? List some potential benefits of conducting a risk management exercise.

5.7.2 Contingencies

Definition

What is the specific difference between a contingency and a risk? Why might some risks be converted to contingency plans during the life of a project?

Example

For the house building project of Question 5.7.1 choose one of the identified contingencies and determine what actions you would take if it came to pass. How might you modify any cost estimates for the project accordingly?

Plan

Consider that you are the manager of the project to implement the warehouse stock control system described in Section 5.4.1. You have been informed that there may be a requirement to use a different make of computer to complete the job because there could be a £5000 cost saving in so doing. The alternative computer is identical to that originally specified but has different power and data cabling requirements and is two feet taller. Make up a suitable, but simple, project plan and modify it to include a contingency plan that covers financial, resource, installation and testing areas of the plan.

5.7.3 External dependencies

Consider again the house building project of Question 5.7.1. For those items that you have defined as external dependencies which are the ones that you think are the highest risk and how might you plan ahead to cope with them? Would you treat them as risks or contingencies?

6   Project management stage 3 – implementation

It is a bad plan that admits of no modification. Publilius Syrus

6.1 Introduction

The implementation stage of the project – the running of the project itself – does not mean that planning has stopped. Indeed, it is an essential part of the project manager's role to review the plan against what is actually happening. A plan that does not reflect reality is of no value whatever. This chapter covers the monitoring, measurement, reporting and change management activities that will form the meat of the workload during the implementation phase of the project life cycle.

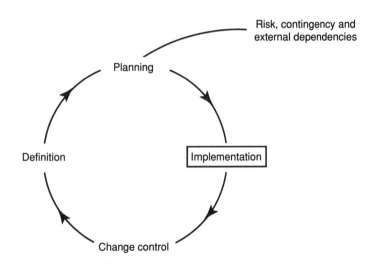

Figure 6.1 Project management process

6.2 Monitoring and control

Once a project is under way the project manager's role changes from start-up to the day-to-day running of the project. This is largely a mechanical exercise combined with the art of listening to what is going on around you.

For instance, you will get reports from each member of the team concerning the progress of their individual work packages. These will probably be either weekly or monthly and will include an indication of how much has been done and how much remains to be done.

You might use some form of work package document (if this formality were deemed necessary), such as the example in Figure 6.2.

Or you might simply ask for the same information to be supplied with a monthly report. However, the collection of the information is important as without it you have no written record or evidence for project progress.

Work package ID	Owner
Title:	Reporting to
Summary/status	
Time spent to date (days) % completed	Time to complete (days)

Figure 6.2 Work package document

6.2.1 Time recording

Related to monitoring and control is time recording and productivity. It is quite common for staff to be required to complete weekly or monthly time sheets where they allocate their time to various project and other tasks. Figure 6.3 shows a typical form that could be used for time sheet recording.

Name: Washington		Month: December - Week 1		Date Completed: 9/12/96					
Activity or Code	Project Name	Mon	Tues	Wed	Thurs	Fri	Sat	Sun	Total
A01				4					4
A02		1.5			3				4.5
A03		3			4.5				7.5
C01		3							3
L01			7.5						7.5
Sales				3.5					3.5
Support									
Holiday						7.5			7.5
Sickness									
Total		7.5	7.5	7.5	7.5	7.5	0	0	37.5

Figure 6.3 Example time sheet

Of course, it is not necessary to use such a low-technology forms-and-hand-writing approach to time recording. It is relatively simple to provide staff with a spreadsheet program that, as a minimum, takes away the need (see also Chapter 7) for adding up the rows and columns. In a network computer environment these can automatically be linked to produce summary sheets for the project manager covering the reported activities of all members of the project team.

Because time sheets are not something that people enjoy filling in, either because they object to the Big Brother associations or because it is boring, it is necessary to find some way of making sure that they are returned on time. Sadly these tend to require some degree of coercion or threat, though more imaginative approaches have been invented. For example, having the expenses claim printed on the rear of the time sheet is one way of encouraging prompt completion, offering a small prize for the person with the best track record – a free drink or meal perhaps on a quarterly basis is another.

Measuring productivity is a controversial subject when it comes to project working. After all, unlike a production line process where you can clearly determine the output of people in terms of widgets per hour etc. there is no simple measure for project work. However, given that most projects are planned in terms of the amount of time that people will have to work to complete individual activities then it follows that the project manager needs to know how much time has been spent by those working on the project. This comes back to some form of time recording/time sheet.

6.2.2 Productivity

Knowing how much time people spend on activities does not mean that you can measure their productivity. Indeed, defining productivity can be a very difficult business in a project environment because, unlike manufacturing, staff are producing work that is a one-off. Consequently there is nothing to compare it with and therefore sensible measurements become difficult. The fundamental truth is that you cannot measure productivity until you have determined what it is you are going to measure.

With this in mind it may be of help to look at specific measures for certain aspects of a project. For example, computer programmers can be measured in terms of lines of finished code completed per day, over the life of the development project. Bricklayers could be measured in terms of courses of brick per day.

However, whilst such measures can be of use for specific individuals in specific roles they are of limited value to project managers. It is the authors' view that the only sensible approach is to take a longer term view and see how staff measure up in terms of delivering what is required against their own commitments to deliver. When it comes down to it what most project managers are concerned with is delivering the project on time and to budget, not measuring specific productivity in terms of measures such as lines of code produced by staff in a month or bricks laid per person per day on a housing estate.

6.3 Performance analysis

As the project progresses it is necessary to assess how the project is going in reality as opposed to what the plan predicted. This is somewhat loosely called performance analysis by the authors, though they acknowledge that this does not stand up to close scrutiny to those more used to a manufacturing environment. Essentially we are talking about how the project is going and how it looks as if it will go in the future.

6.3.1 Actual versus planned

The simplest measure is the historic comparison of planned time to complete an activity versus the actual time taken. For each completed activity on the plan a record is kept of how long it took to complete compared with the planned time. Figure 6.4 shows how this can be measured on a Gantt chart comparing the original plan against what has actually been achieved. In this case the project has slipped by two days.

The original plan is shown on the lower of the two bars for each task. The percentage indicators show how much of each task has been completed. As usual the arrows indicate the linking of tasks – where the late finishing of one task delays the start of a subsequent one.

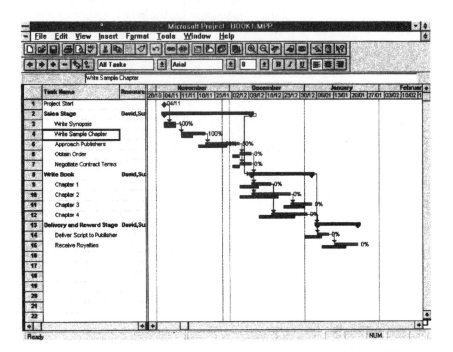

Figure 6.4 Sample project Gantt chart

Milestones

Milestones are also useful when monitoring progress and the same techniques may be used when measuring time to go/percentage of the work completed before a particular milestone is completed. Note that a milestone is not an activity in itself, it is merely an indicator that a particular stage in the project has been reached. However, as stated in earlier chapters, milestones often have payments associated with them and so it can be very important to monitor them carefully.

6.3.2 Forecasting

There are many theories about forecasting, some seem more scientific than others. However, the reality of it is that forecasting is an art rather than a science. Curiously it is often considered harder to forecast small projects than it is to forecast large projects. The reason for this is largely statistical and the author's own experience of a small project for a telecommunication company will serve as an example.

The project involved four people, two full, time one part time, and was managed by the author on a part-time basis. The project was well defined and should have been straightforward to complete within a two to three month time frame. Initially all went well and it seemed that it would go to budget and time without any difficulties. Then one of the full-time staff fell of the platform of a bus, breaking his leg. This effectively removed him from the picture for the expected duration of the project. Next the other full-time staff member had appendicitis – things were starting to look bad. Fortunately the customer had a major delay with another supplier which would have held the project up badly so it seemed that all was well and once the bus victim had returned to work things seemed to be running well again. However, the returnee was of Australian stock and, sadly his father died unexpectedly and he had to return to his homeland to sort things out. No one is likely to be able to forecast this scale of disaster on a small-scale project of this nature – it was just unusually bad luck.

If you are managing a larger project with, say, 20 people working over a period of a year or more then these types of problem tend to average themselves out over the lifetime of the project. You are unlikely to have 10 broken legs, dying parents overseas, etc. and the other swings and roundabouts of project life will tend to be spread evenly over the project. You will find that forecasts behave somewhat more predictably, though this does not mean that life will be easy!

In the case of a project where there are clearly activities that are not on the critical path for completing the project it is tempting to concentrate only on forecasts for the critical activities and leave the rest to themselves. This is a mistake, a small overrun on a non-critical activity can soon make it into a critical one.

Typically you should expect to update your Gantt/PERT chart to your current forecast on a monthly basis This will allow you to see any trends that are developing.

6.3.3 Simple forecasting methods	There are two simple and commonly used ways of asking people to forecast how their work is going - one is percentage completed and the other is time to complete.
Percentage completed	People are requested to give an estimate of how complete their tasks are, e.g. 50 per cent, 80 per cent, 100 per cent (when completed). The project manager then uses this as a basis to calculate when completion will occur. Although simple, this method has a fundamental flaw based on an unofficial law known as the 80/20 rule. It is generally thought that 80 per cent of any task gets done in the first 20 per cent of the time and that the remaining 20 per cent takes the remaining 80 per cent. Possibly this is because people naturally tend to get all the easy work done first, which they do quickly, leaving the difficult problems, which take longer, until the end. Consequently, reports of percentage completed are subject to optimistic forecasting initially and then what will seem like pessimistic forecasting as the task nears completion. For this reason percentage completion is not recommended as the preferred method. Many project management packages are based on percentage completed reporting. However, this does not mean that the raw material has to be gathered in this way.
Time to complete	This is perhaps rather more reliable than percentage to complete. Here the information requested is, when will the task be finished? This requires a certain amount of trust to be invested in the project staff and this is no bad thing. If you do not have this trust in the project team then it brings into question the overall health of the team working environment. By asking when the project is complete you avoid the 80/20 problem and rely on people providing a realistic estimate of when their task will be completed. Of course the experience of the staff needs to be taken into account here, those for whom this is their first exposure to project work may have a poor grasp as to what completion means. In particular they may be unaware of all the boring bits, such as documentation, testing etc. that are involved in a real project as opposed to just doing a straight technical/specialist job. In the case of such staff then some assistance or training must be provided to allow them to come up with a realistic estimate. This training and mentoring effort should have been built into the project timetable when producing the original plan (see Chapter 4).

It is the view of the authors that this time-to-complete approach is the preferred one for the reasons stated above.

6.3.4 Financial forecasting

The other side of forecasting is concerned with financial issues. In part this is a follow on from forecasting project completion, largely concerned with how much work people need to do to complete the work. In other words you just add up the number of days/hours of work required to complete the project and multiply by the labour rates that apply. However, that is not the complete story – there is also the need to look at material and equipment costs.

As with the labour costs, the project manager needs to get estimates and forecasts from the people performing the individual activities and then roll this up to produce a forecast for the project as a whole.

In addition there needs to be a reconciliation between the money that goes out from the project with that which comes in from the customer in terms of cash flow. Typically the project will spend money monthly or weekly on labour costs/equipment hire and as invoiced for materials and equipment purchased outright. Income will be based on 'milestone' and contract related payments.

For example consider a project to install a computerized stock control system for a builder's merchant. There might be a payment on signing the order (say 10 per cent), a payment on agreeing the detailed design (25 per cent), then on delivery (50 per cent) with a final payment after the system had operated successfully for 6 months (15 per cent). Financial forecasting for income would then depend entirely on the timing of the project meeting the payment milestones. Forecasting for expenditure would depend on the labour and capital expenditure as determined by the current (i.e. updated) project plan.

6.3.5 Problem identification

An important task for the project manager is the early identification of problems, so that in an ideal world they can be solved before they impact the project. In this section we are concerned with physical problems such as technical problems delaying progress, jobs turning out to be more complex than expected, estimates proving to be optimistic, etc. Problems relating to staff conflicts, poor delegation skills, unclear communication etc. and with third party suppliers, are covered in Chapters 8, 9, 10 and 11.

Classic symptoms of projects going wrong are tasks which are continually reported as being 'nearly' complete but which keep having effort spent on them with no apparent change in the degree of completion or tasks for which the forecast completion date moves forward at the same rate as work is done.
Similarly issues which keep being reported as requiring attention but never seem to go away indicate underlying problems which may not be being revealed.

6.3.6 Corrective actions

All the problems that are likely to come out of the problem identification in Section 6.3.3. will tend to result in project slippage and related overspend. There are five frequently used corrective actions available to the project manager: rearrange the workload, use more effort, increase the workload, change the scope or quality of the deliverable and change the completion date. These are covered in more detail below.

1 **Rearrange the workload.** Where one task is in trouble it may be possible to rearrange some of the other tasks, particularly those further off the critical path, to allow more effort to be spent on the task that is running late. This approach may require some re-planning but this is worthwhile if it brings the project back into schedule. Of course, a tightly planned project – most of them

are nowadays – may not allow this to happen as there will be no spare effort to help out, see also the cautionary note in Item 2.

2 **Use more effort (men in hole).** Here the idea is that getting in some temporary help – either from within the organization or from an external temporary/contract agency – will get you through the short-term problem. This has cost implications for the project and, as with rearranging the workload, it may well be that the project cannot run to this. In addition, this approach can suffer from the 'digging a hole' problem. There are only so many people you can get in a hole to dig it at a given time without them getting in each other's way. However, there may well be some aspects of the task, such as documentation, that can be separated out, allowing the main task to receive more concentration from the person responsible for its completion.

3 **Increase workload (overtime).** This is the other side of the 'use more effort' approach. Here the idea is to obtain the additional effort from within the project team by asking for overtime or extended hours working. This will typically have cost implications in the same way that using temporary staff has.

4 **Change the scope/quality constraints.** Negotiation is the name of the game for this (see Chapter 8). The intention is to change what is to be supplied or the quality constraints that apply to it.

5 **Move the completion date.** This is the default! If you don't do anything the completion date will slip. However, it may be possible to re-negotiate this with the client and it is much easier to do this earlier rather than it coming as a surprise a couple of days before the project is due to complete. Negotiating this may well revert to changing the scope of the delivery as discussed in Item 4 above.

6.4 Reporting

Reporting is another activity which makes demands on a project manager's time. It is inevitable, and not unreasonable, that those who are paying for a project will want some sort of written record of what is going on and how the project is progressing against the original plan.

6.4.1 Report writing

Report: *A document or communication presenting information on a specified subject.*
Project managers are going to write reports for customers, suppliers, their own management and for the project team themselves.

There are four questions which you should ask yourself, and answer, before you write a single word:

- Who is going to read the document?
- What are the objectives for the report?
- What are the key points?
- What is the best structure?

Of these the first comes down to 'Know your audience' – you must write your report in a way that is both easy to understand and relevant to their needs. Related to this, a serious consideration for report writers is the non-interactive nature of the beast. You will not have the opportunity to answer questions in person about what you write, similarly you will not have the opportunity to change the way or level in which the information is presented, as you might in a presentation.

Consequently you must find out as much as possible about this audience. The following checklist will help you:

- What are their interests?
- Is English their first language (particularly important in multinational companies/projects)?
- Are they technical/business/non-specialist people?
- Are they decision makers?
- Can they gain anything from it?
- What do they really want/need to know?

The reason that their interests are listed as the first point is because it has a significant impact on the way you treat the answers to the other points. People are more comfortable with words and concepts that they use all the time and are consequently more receptive to reports that use these words. Of course there are limits to this; a report may be targeted at more than one group within the total audience – but you can still make sure that it takes account of all who will read it even if this means adopting a more complex document structure to do so.

The second point relates to your objectives for the report. A strict objective may be given to you, e.g. a monthly financial report showing project spend versus budget for the project. Such a report could consist of straightforward facts with no conclusions or predictions. However, in practice project reports have a wider brief and objectives will be broader and will include both those of the audience and those of the project team and the customer as well.

The third point is more analytical. You may well have a large amount of information at your disposal and it requires the exercise of judgement to decide what to include and what to leave out. One way of doing this is to look at what you have available and decide what is relevant to the audience using the information you gleaned from point one. Of course, in the case of weekly and monthly reports you will soon find out if you have left anything out because someone will tell you! However, you are unlikely to get any feedback on irrelevant information; people will think it is relevant to someone else if not to them. The maxim should be, 'if in doubt, leave it out'.

The last point is structure. This is very important; a badly constructed report may well have all the facts in it, and contain useful recommendations and conclusions, but if they are scattered willy-nilly then it is a fair bet they will be ignored. Again, knowing the audience will almost certainly tell you that badly organized, rambling discourses don't go down well with the typical purchaser of high-value projects!

A good starting point is actually what was traditionally taught at school: 'Say what you're going to say, say it, say what you've said', i.e. summarize the key points first (management summary), then proceed to sections with the core information (relegate very detailed information to appendices if it threatens to dilute the message), and then present a conclusion which combines key facts with any recommendations.

Report contents

1 Introduction
2 Summary
3 Body of the report
4 Conclusion
5 Appendices.

Specifically:

- **Introduction:** Describe what the report is for, who the target audience is (especially if it is a one-off report), give an overview of the structure of the report (if it is lengthy), and where the information can be found.

- **Summary:** List the main points of the report, preferably in the order they are presented in the main body of the document. Where appropriate it should include a summary of the conclusions as well.
- **Main report:** A series of sections, chapters, or whatever is appropriate for the scale of the report, which include the information in sufficient detail to meet the requirements of the reader.
- **Conclusion:** All the conclusions/recommendations and key facts should be pulled together in a logical fashion to underline the import of the report.
- **Appendices:** Background and specialist information in detail to support the main body of the report or to cover special interest readers. Typically this includes technical, statistical or legal material that would be either too long or too specialist to include elsewhere.

6.4.2 Progress reports

Except for the smallest and shortest of projects there will be a requirement for regular, possibly frequent, progress reports. Although all the points about reports in general given above apply, they are worth considering in their own right. The reports serve as a formal documentation of what is happening in the project. There are a range of people who may need to receive these within an organization such as accountants, senior management, logistical support groups, personnel, sales and marketing. A key point concerning project reports is that they should not contain surprises for the recipient, they are largely a matter of record – the good project manager will have made sure that those that need to know, and are affected by issues and changes, will have been made party to the decisions/information before they are impacted by them.

Following the general structures outlined in Section 6.4.1, a typical progress report would cover the following: summary; achievements; issues, escalations; and forecast.

- **Summary:** Key points arising from the reporting period's activity. A snapshot of the state of the project, is it on schedule, budget, major issues, etc.
- **Achievements:** Milestones that have been met, activities and tasks that have been completed, issues resolved.
- **Issues:** Sometimes a euphemism for problems. Specific items that require action either to prevent a problem occurring or resolve an existing one.
- **Escalations:** Issues that require action from a higher level within the organization or the customer.
- **Forecast:** Estimates for the forthcoming reporting period of spend, time to completion, milestones that will be completed, etc.

6.4.3 Customer reports

The nature of these reports could well be defined as being a project deliverable at the start of the project. They can take a variety of forms from simple minutes of progress meetings to formal reports delivered on a weekly or monthly basis.

A typical customer report will cover much the same ground as a progress report but will be geared to the needs of the client. Unlike internal reports it will not normally include information about supplier specific financial issues and you would always expect problems to be associated with a solution.

However, one thing that you should never do in a customer report – if you do it will be at your own peril – is cover up a problem or an issue. It is always better to flag up snags when they are small than to disguise them and get discovered once they are serious. The betrayal of trust which occurs when you are not honest with the customer is hard or impossible to repair.

Monthly Report Number 3 – Period 01 November to 30 November 1996

Project: Business units

Customer: Grange Farm Restorations

Project manager:

Date of report: 3 December 1996

Summary
The main site has now been cleared and work is progressing well on the drainage, basic services and access road foundations. The work on building the perimeter walls/fencing has been delayed by a general shortage of the stone cladding specified by the architects – this is under review and is expected to be resolved within the next two weeks. Spend is ahead of the nominal budget, but this is due to purchasing certain materials in advance of requirements to take advantage of the opportunity to purchase bankrupt stock from a building merchant. Site security may have to be increased in the light of recent petty thefts and the threat this implies for the storage of these materials.

Achievements
The site clearance has been completed.

Failure of Bodgit Ltd. has allowed the purchase of the brick, stone, breeze block materials to be purchased at a substantial discount (40%) of the original budget. This saving is offset by 5% due to interest charges that will be incurred on the borrowing required to fund it.

Issues
The brick laying sub-contractor Grundy and Co. have ceased to trade owing to termination of their lease by their landlord. They have been unable to find new premises and were unable to afford rented accommodation.

Petty crime has been encountered on the site out of hours (theft of some building materials and a cement mixer). In order to protect the large stock of materials that have been purchased at beneficial cost it has been decided to employ a security company to provide out-of-hours cover. The cost of this is still less than 30% of the savings that have been realized by this purchase (inclusive of borrowing charges).

There is a shortage of the cladding materials required for the perimeter wall. This is being addressed with the architects to see if a larger panel size can be used whilst maintaining the same colour/texture. The originals specified are no longer in manufacture in the non-metric size format, but are available in the larger metric form.

Escalations
Permission is required to either appoint one of the original tenderers (at higher cost than Grundy and Co.) or to accept the delay, and consequent expenses that would be required to find a new sub-contractor.

Forecast
It is expected that the project will be on schedule, as originally planned, by the end of the current financial quarter. The financial forecast is that, due to the advance purchases outlined above, the project should be under budget at the halfway stage, though provisions may have to be made to cover increased labour costs if a replacement for the bricklaying company cannot be obtained at the same price as Grundy and Co. who have gone out of business.

Figure 6.5 Example progress report

The internal report of Section 6.4.2 could be reproduced for customer consumption looking something like Figure 6.6.

Monthly Report Number 3 - Period 01 November to 30 November 1996

Project: Business units

Customer: Grange Farm Restorations

Project manager:

Date of report: 3 December 1996

Summary
The main site has now been cleared and work is progressing well on the drainage, basic services and access road foundations. The work on building the perimeter walls/fencing has been delayed by approximately two weeks due to the requirement to choose a metric cladding material owing to the non-availability of the imperial material originally specified. This is not expected to impact the overall project time scale. Site security is under review and will probably be increased in the light of recent petty theft.

Achievements
The site clearance has been completed.

Issues
Currently obtaining new estimates for brick laying suppliers to replace Grundy and Co. Petty crime has been encountered on the site out of hours (theft of some building materials and a cement mixer). Increased site security required.

Escalations
Permission is required to either appoint one of the original tenderers (at higher cost than Grundy and Co.) or to accept a delay of about two weeks, and consequent expenses, estimated at £1200, that would be required to find a new sub-contractor.

Forecast
It is expected that the project will be completed on schedule, provided that either an agreed increase in price for the cladding materials to fund purchase of more expensive materials or the effort needed to find an alternative supplier in the time scale is accepted.

Figure 6.6 Example customer report

6.4.4 Financial reports

Another type of report is the financial one. These tend to be specific to the organization involved and can be quite complex. Typically they would include spend to date versus planned spend, cash flow, forecast spend, revenue versus cost information, forecast profit and loss, borrowing requirements and related measures. These may well be related to particular time periods (months/quarters/financial years) rather than the project life cycle. The organization concerned will make it clear what is required and, in the most part, the rest will be a mechanical exercise deriving the numbers form the basic project progress information recorded from time sheets. Where a project manager is running more than one project he or she may be required to summarize their cumulative financial impact on the organization as well as individual numbers. It is worth noting that many financial reports are highly confidential and it should be established what their circulation should be.

An example of a financial report is given in Figure 6.7.

Monthly Internal Financial Report for the Grundy project

1 Summary
2 Spend to date/current month

Total project spend to date (Oct 12 to Dec 30) £21,050
Current month   (Dec 1 to Dec 30)   £12,075

3 Revenue to date/current month
Total   (Oct 12 to Dec 30) £16,000 (initial payment)
Current month   (Dec 1 to Dec 30)   £0 (no scheduled payment)

4 Cash flow current financial quarter
Negative cash flow of £5075

5 Forecast for project and financial year (£)

	Oct	Nov	Dec	Jan	Feb	Mar
In	16,000	0	0	10,000	0	20,000
Out	2,300	6,675	12,075	12,500	8,000	2,500
Balance	13,700	7,025	−5,075	−7,575	−15,757	1,743

Figure 6.7 Example financial report

6.5 The project file

During the implementation stage of the project cycle it is all too easy to get bored with maintaining the project file. The wise project manager will not allow this to happen and will place copies of all the reports covered in Section 6.4 in this file. It is also particularly important to make sure that this file includes updated copies of project plans and estimates. It is quite common to find that the project plan in the file is the first one that was produced when the project was defined and planed. Six months later this bears little resemblance to what is actually happening and the latest version of the plan. Put aside a fixed time, perhaps a Friday, each week to check that the file is up to date and remind people of its existence and importance from time to time (see also Chapter 3 for definition of project file contents).

6.6 Change

One of the realities of projects is that things change; the odds on a project – even a very small one – going from start to finish without changes to one or all of objectives, time scale or budget are very long indeed. Project managers spend a significant part of their time managing change.

The definition, planning, implementation approach applies just as well to changes as it does to projects at the high level. Effectively a change is a mini project in its own right. You need to define what is required, what it will cost, what resources are needed, the impact on time scales, produce a plan, and implement it in much the same way as you would a complete project.

6.6.1 Change request

Changes may be initiated for a wide variety of reasons:

- new technology becomes available;
- budgets may be changed;
- customer requirements may change;
- completion dates may be brought forward;
- tasks may prove to take longer/shorter than expected.

For large projects it is conventional to have some formal process for logging, approving and implementing changes. It may be necessary to have a change control committee whose job is to investigate the overall impact of a change to one part of a project on another, etc.

Whatever the size of the project, it is useful to have a simple form to record and control change requests and log their progress from request to implementation. Figure 6.8 shows such a form. The key points are that it provides a reference number for tracking purposes, records who asked for the change and when, what the change is, why it is being requested and provides space for recording the cost and time scales associated with its implementation and the formal approval to go ahead (or not!).

Change Request Form (Version 1.0)			
Requested by:	Date requested:	Date reviewed:	Log number:
Description (attach additional pages if required)			
Reason for change request			
Cost estimate		Time estimate	
Approved (Y/N) Signature		Date	

Figure 6.8 Example change form

As mentioned, it is a good idea to maintain a change log which records receipt of change requests, whether they are accepted or rejected and the date of that decision.

6.6.2 Change definition

The first step in change management is defining the scope of the change. Once a change request has been received it needs to be defined in sufficient detail to allow it to be implemented.

Note: If changes are very large then it can become a costly exercise defining and evaluating them – in this case the project manager may need to agree with the customer who is going to pay for this activity. In the case of large projects this may well have been agreed as part of the negotiation of terms and conditions of supply.

6.6.3 Change planning

Once the change has been defined it is necessary to produce a plan for implementing it together with the estimated cost.

6.6.4 Change risk assessment

As was done during the definition and planning stages it is necessary to assess the risks associated with the change.

6.6.5 Change implementation

Finally, once a change has been agreed with the customer or the sponsoring organization, etc., then the change is incorporated into the overall plan and gets implemented along with the rest of the project.

6.7 Summary

This chapter has covered the daily toil of the project manager – what happens once the project is up and running after all the start-up and up-front planning activities have been completed. This is the bread and butter of the project manager's lot. The work breaks down into three main areas: monitoring; managing change; and reporting. For most projects this is the longest stage of the project during which the largest numbers of people will be involved.

6.8 Exercises

6.8.1 Monitoring and control

Design a time sheet for a software development project. How might you ensure that the time sheet is completed on time? What non-project specific elements would you account for?

6.8.2 Performance analysis

Consider a project for painting all the rooms in a large school building during the summer holiday period (i.e. when the building is not in use). Six painters are involved and the project should last five weeks. How might you assess the productivity of the painters? If the original plan assumed that one painter could paint one wall in two hours and you find that some painters do better than this, some worse, how might you forecast the actual completion date of the project after the end of the first week?

6.8.3 Report writing

Write a report detailing progress to date on a project you are familiar with – if you are not currently involved in one make one up or write one about your progress to date with your current training courses. Initially write this report for the 'project team', then re-write it for a customer and/or your immediate superior.

Write a financial status report for a project you are involved in, or make one up for a project to produce a prototype hedge-trimmer.

6.8.4 Project file

Why is it important to keep this file up to date? What are the potential problems that might arise from failing to do this? What strategies might you adopt to help keep the file up to date?

6.8.5 Change control

You are the manager of a project to produce a prototype agricultural hedge trimmer. This device was originally specified to be operated by one person using a small petrol engine. As it is for agricultural use the device has been specified to be rugged, efficient and compliant with safety regulations but there has been no emphasis on quietness. The marketing department has decided that there is a domestic market for such a machine in place of the top-of-the-range electric powered machines. This would be mainly for those who had very large gardens with large hedges where it is impractical to use either a mains lead or a rechargeable system. However, to meet the needs of this market they have requested that you produce a version with an add-on extra silencer to make noise levels acceptable. Produce a simple project plan for producing the prototype and show how it might need to be changed to incorporate the new requirement. Produce sample change documentation in historical sequence that shows how you might go from change request to implementation. What factors would you consider when assessing the acceptability of the change? If you prefer a non-engineering example, consider a change request to a children's playground to give improved wheelchair access.

7   Tools and techniques

Give us the tools and we'll do the job. Winston Churchill.

The tools and techniques that are available to the project manager cover a wide spectrum. The goal of this chapter is to provide the reader with an introduction to what to expect and a grounding in the vocabulary of project management techniques.

7.1 Introduction

Project managers need to organize large amounts of information and determine how different items relate to each other. So for as long as there have been project managers there have been tools designed to help them to this job more easily. It probably started with the chief hunter, 'Erk' getting everyone together and making sure they all had their stone axes and spears, enough drinking water and some idea where they were going to hunt for food. He, or she, had a clear goal for the team, had identified the resources required to do the job and the method by which the goal was to be achieved. The principal project management tool was probably a bigger axe than anyone else had! Since those times things have moved on somewhat, though not noticeably if some organizations are to go by, and there are a large variety of tools available to the project manager.

This chapter provides an overview of some of the more commonly used methods and techniques available today. How these techniques are used in different working environments tends to be specific to the company organization involved. In addition, there are many detail differences between individual implementations of each method. Consequently, the intention is to provide the reader with the ability to recognize them and gain a basic understanding of what to expect from them and understand what can be achieved.

The chapter covers the most common methods and tools including Gantt charts, work breakdown structures (WBS), PERT, critical path analysis and how computer-based tools make life easier for the project manager. One of the benefits of using these de facto standard tools, and the reason for their choice for this book, is that other people can understand them and thus they can become effective communication aids for all those involved with a project, both inside and outside the project team itself.

7.2 Gantt charts

The simplest project management tool of all is the shopping list. It tells you what resources you need and you cross them off until you have everything ready for the weekend's eating and drinking. What it doesn't tell you, however, is when you need these things, and in what order and which items become useless without some of the others.

A simple way of remedying these short comings is to turn the list into one axis of an XY graph and make time the other one. Then you can put start and end dates against each item. In addition you can write down next to the activities who is going to be responsible for doing them. The chart tells you what is going to be done, when and by whom. Take this one step further and group related tasks together and you have what is commonly called a Gantt chart (after Henry Gantt who promoted its use around the end of the nineteenth century). Figure 7.1 shows a typical Gantt chart for a small project to write a book.

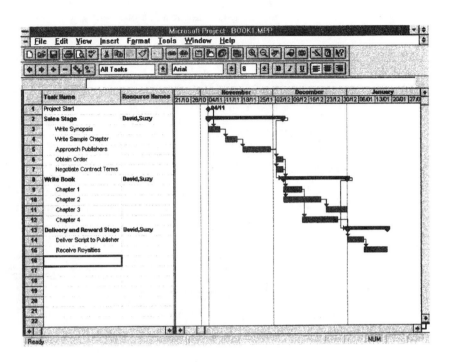

Figure 7.1 Gantt chart

For small projects Gantt charts can conveniently show links between tasks, representing where one must end before another commences, by linking them with arrows. In the example it is considered necessary to sell the book before you starting it.

This is all very well for planning the project, but what about reporting progress? Well, this is straightforward too. If you draw the boxes hollow to start with then you can fill them in as they are completed. This gives a simple, at a glance representation of how things are going. If an activity hasn't started or been finished by the right day it is visually very obvious that something is awry. Figure 7.2 shows how a computer-based application shows progress.

Figure 7.2 Gantt chart showing milestones

You can easily do all this just using a piece of paper and a pencil – the minimum tool kit for the budding project manager! However, as we've established, projects have to be continually re-planned at time passes to take into account changes to the project and the effect of external and unforeseen events. Of course you can simply redraw the plan each time this happens and for a small project this is not much a of a limitation. But once projects get above a certain size this becomes impractical; you would be spending all your time at the drawing board and none of your time managing the project, unless you are using a suitable computer based system to do the donkey work for you. These systems don't do anything that you couldn't do yourself, but they make it very much quicker and their ability to manipulate the information quickly allows you the luxury of 'what-if' planning.

7.2.1 Milestones

Another feature of Gantt charts is the ease with which you can identify milestones, key events in the development of the project such as receipt of order, agreement of design specification, delivery of finished product, etc. You simply make a suitable mark on the plan, thus fixing the date of the milestone and its relationship to other activities. Figure 7.3 shows the project start milestone (see also Chapter 4).

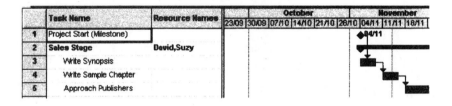

	Task Name	Resource Names		October						November		
			23/09	30/09	07/10	14/10	21/10	26/10	04/11	11/11	18/11
1	Project Start (Milestone)								◆04/11		
2	Sales Stage	David,Suzy									
3	Write Synopsis										
4	Write Sample Chapter										
5	Approach Publishers										

Figure 7.3 Example project start milestone

7.2.2 Disadvantages of Gantt

A weakness of the Gantt chart in the simplest form is that of resource planning. Although you have identified who does what you also need to make sure that you haven't allocated more than 100 per cent of someone's time to the project – all too easy to do when there are hundreds of individual tasks allocated across a project team. Obviously this is not such a problem with small teams where the manager knows each individual's workload because they talk to them every day. There is also an issue with display sequential information – where one task is dependent on the completion of another. As stated, this is OK with small projects where you can just use a few arrows as links, but it can become very confusing on large projects. There are ways round this, for example, having hierarchical families of Gantt charts, but for larger projects this can become confusing where dependencies are concerned.

The Gantt chart is consequently most suitable when being used for small to medium sized projects with up to a dozen or so people working on them.

7.2.3 Gantt summary

Such charts are very popular and most computer-based project tools support them. Project manager's Workbench produced by Hoskyns was one of the first PC-based tools on the market and the early versions were almost entirely based upon the use of Gantt charts as the means of displaying the state of a project. Most computer-based packages will allow the project to be viewed as a Gantt chart.

- Easy to understand – visually very clear.
- Easy to produce – can be done with pencil and graph paper.
- Over-allocation or resource difficult to see.
- Dependencies can be hard to identify.

7.3 Work breakdown structure (WBS)

Anything but the smallest of projects is difficult to understand unless it is broken down into readily comprehensible sub-units. One of the most common ways of doing this is known as the work breakdown structure. These typically use three or more levels of structure, though the actual number will vary according to the size and complexity of the project. These levels are hierarchical, and serve to allow a complex project to be broken down into manageable components, the bottom level having the rule that only one person can be allocated to a task.

A three-level system might consist of process, activity and task. For example, you might break down the process of producing a new domestic appliance into high-level activities of design, development, testing and production. These in turn might be split up into their own components: for example design including electrical design, physical design and mechanical design.

Figure 7.4 shows various levels of detail in a WBS for a house building project. Once all the individual tasks have been identified it is then possible to associate skills, resources and costs to each one. This makes WBS a very useful means of costing a project and establishing, once it is in progress, the spend to date and the forecast cost to completion (sometimes known as FCC). This is covered in more detail in Chapter 3 project definition.

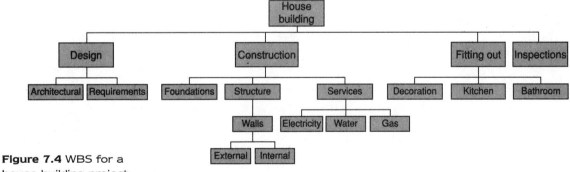

Figure 7.4 WBS for a house building project

WBS shows what is to be done and how work is to be broken down into groups of activities. It does not show dependencies or time scale.

Whatever you call it, the bottom level of any plan must have the feature that each individual job has only one person responsible for getting it done. It is acceptable for one person to be responsible for several jobs, it is not acceptable for two or more people to be responsible for a single job. This is essential if you are going to avoid the situation where person A says 'I thought B was doing it,' then B says, 'No, A is doing it,' the result being that nobody does the work. This ripples up through the plan – you have one individual who is in overall responsibility for a group of tasks, even if the individual tasks are allocated to a number of people. These individuals are often referred to by the term 'team leader'.

7.4 PERT

Next to Gantt charts PERT is one of the most common project management tools. It was originally developed in the 1960s by Lockheed Aircraft Corporation for the Polaris Missile System project. It stands for project evaluation and review technique. Lockheed estimate that its use saved two years during the development of this project. Prior to this there was a rumour that when a ship got built they used to line up all the tradesmen along the side of the deck and whoever got there first had a straight run with their pipe or cable and everyone else had to bend theirs round it! As electricians are generally thinner and fitter than plumbers this meant that little thin cables would go in straight lines and then large steam pipes would get bent round them. Very amusing for the electricians but very inefficient in terms of getting the ship fitted quickly.

7.4.1 PERT basics

PERT charts show activities usually represented as boxes whose relationships to each other are shown by links, represented as arrows/lines. The boxes are also known as 'nodes'. Figure 7.5 shows the information included on a typical PERT node. There are other ways of displaying this information, as can be seen on the book writing project example.

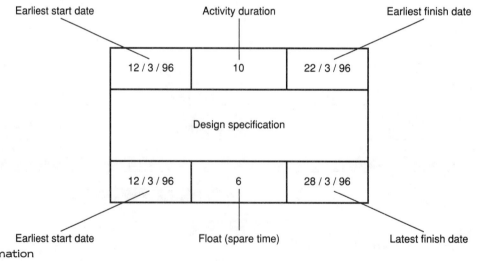

Figure 7.5 Information on a typical PERT node

The example PERT chart shown in Figure 7.6 is a PERT view of the Gantt chart for writing a book shown in Figure 7.1. It is immediately apparent that PERT is very good for showing the way tasks in a project are interlinked and how they fit together to form the project as a whole.

7.4.2 Critical path analysis (CPA)

This term was originally coined for use with PERT charts (though it really applies to any project planning methods based on tasks), and referred to the identification of the critical path (i.e. the shortest timed activities) for getting the project done. Those activities which are on the critical path can be given closer scrutiny. Essentially it consists of establishing which activities have to be completed first at any stage of the project for it to finish on time.

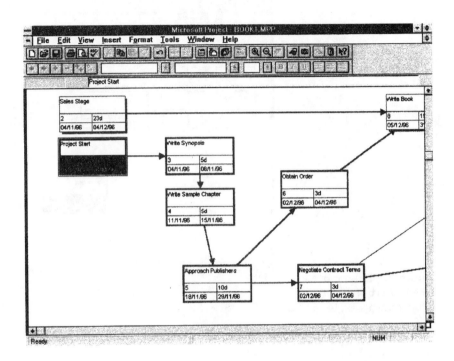

Figure 7.6 PERT chart

For example at one instant in time you might have three activities happening simultaneously which all have to be completed before the next stage of the project can begin. If one of these takes longer than the other two then it is said to be on the 'critical path'. The PERT chart shown in Figure 7.7 shows such a situation. In most PERT and Gantt displays on computer-based packages there is a facility to highlight the critical path either in a particular colour, by enhancing the surrounding lines or by putting the text into bold highlight.

In Figure 7.7 you can see that the design activity is not on the critical path but the procure land activity is. This is shown by the thicker line and box surrounding the activity.

Before computers, calculating critical paths for large projects required an army of clerks to complete a single analysis for a large project. However, it is now a relatively trivial activity even on a modest PC system, and 'what if' modelling where different amounts of resources are considered for each task can be considered to determine the most suitable way to run the project.

7.4.3 Critical activities

PERT charts indicate the activities that are 'critical' by use of colour, or some other form of highlighting. These are defined as those activities that must be completed on time if the project is to run to schedule.

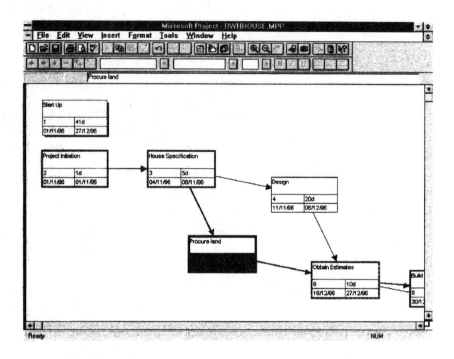

Figure 7.7 Example PERT chart showing critical path

7.4.4 Float

When you talk to people about PERT you find they keep talking about float. Essentially what they are doing is saying how much spare time there is for an activity. This is defined in terms of the time available to do the task and the time required to complete it. Negative float means the project is going to be late. Positive float means it probably wasn't scheduled aggressively enough. You can't win!

7.4.5 Disadvantages of PERT

The main disadvantage of PERT is that the network and nodes (boxes) are simply not as visually clear as the bars on a Gantt chart.

Also, for anything larger than a small project the charts can become incomprehensible as the network of activities grows and the interlinking becomes ever more complex. It is not uncommon to find whole office walls covered with a PERT chart.

PERT does not make it easy to see who is supposed to be doing what and in that respect it is inferior to Gantt charts. Typically you have to have a WBS or equivalent in addition to PERT to take care of this side of the project.

7.4.6 PERT summary

PERT is a very powerful and popular technique and it would be very surprising if anyone involved with project work on a long-term basis did not come into contact with it at some point in their career. Their main strength lies in the simple representation of the sequence of events that must take place in completing a project. Although simple to grasp in principle, PERT charts for large projects can become very unwieldy and difficult to comprehend at a glance. But they do lend themselves to what ifs and forecasting completion dates.

PERT is a powerful and flexible tool but requires some knowledge before it is really useful.

7.5 Project scheduling

Another area where project tools are useful is in project scheduling. At its simplest scheduling is simply allocating tasks to people. In a small project there is little scope for changing the order in which things get done; task b naturally follows on from task a and so on to the end of the project. Furthermore there is likely to be little flexibility for sharing the load between different team members as only certain members of the team have the relevant skills to do particular tasks. However, in larger projects where there are significant numbers of parallel activities there can be many permutations of sequence and order in carrying out the activities needed to complete the job. Similarly there are issues with how resources are to be utilized – do you want to get the job done as quickly as possible regardless of cost? Is time of no great importance? What level of quality control is required? This is another aspect of the 'good, quick, cheap' job theory; you can only have any two of these within the same job. However, the way you resource and schedule a job will be dependent on what the time/resource/quality constraints apply to it. There are two main criteria employed in project resourcing: resource-limited scheduling and time-limited scheduling. To illustrate this we have produced two version of the same project which show the effect on time scale and cost.

7.5.1 Resource-limited scheduling

With this approach the idea is to schedule the project to use the minimum of staff resources possible. This corresponds to the lowest cost – i.e. cheapest – option. Here tasks are shared evenly between all the members of the team so that they are all optimally utilized over the length of the project. This means that tasks will be delayed so that they fit with staff available. Figure 7.8 shows the project plan. The cost for this option is £X, the time scale is £Y.

Three resources (Designer 1, Technical 1 and Technical 2) are used so that they are all used as efficiently as possible – this gives the lowest cost, but extends the time scale somewhat.

7.5.2 Time-limiting project scheduling

Time-limited scheduling (Figure 7.9) is based on getting the job done in the minimum amount of time, with the assumption that the resource is available to support it, in this case the addition of the resource Technical 3. This leads to a higher-cost option than the resource-limited example given in Figure 7.8, but produces a project to a specific time scale.

Of course, whatever the resource available there are finite limits to what can be achieved – you can only get so many people in a hole digging at the same time before they get in each other's way. There is a minimum time for any task which cannot be improved upon.

7.5.3 Scheduling in the real world

In practice real projects are seldom, if ever, scheduled in either of these methods alone. Compromise is the order of the day and there will be constraints on time, cost and quality which will make demands on the scheduling of the project. The project manager will need to tune the scheduling of the

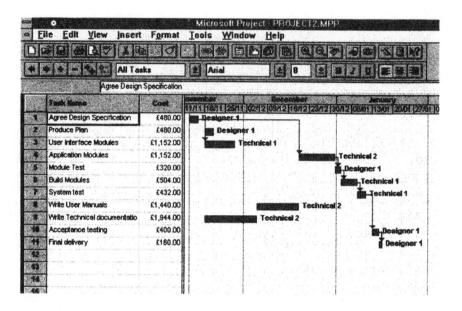

Figure 7.8 Resource-limited project scheduling

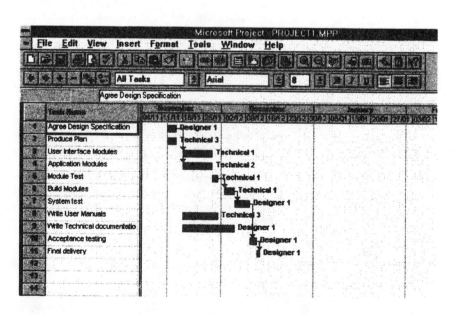

Figure 7.9 Time-limited project scheduling

work to get the best match with these constraints. In the past this would have taken a significant amount of time; today PC-based packages are sufficiently powerful to enable a project manager to try a large number of permutations in a very short period of time. The end result is likely to be a series of compromises with some parts of the project resourced for speed – probably those on the critical path – and others scheduled for economy. External factors largely beyond the project manager's control will determine the overall schedule that you end up with.

7.6 Computer-based tools

The mechanical nature of project planning makes it a natural for computer assistance. Indeed, since the 1960s computers have been pressed into supporting project management, making it one of the first non-financial or scientific applications. The advent of the mass market PC in the early 1980s brought about a revolution in the tools available to the project manager.

Initially tools provided only one method of defining and measuring a project, for example with only the ability to display the results as a Gantt chart. However, it is now reasonable to expect a PC to produce Gantt and PERT charts and perform critical path analyses without having to go for an outlandishly expensive package. Furthermore, many packages will allow you to view the same project data using different methods, thus allowing you to take advantages of the good points of different approaches without being limited by the deficiencies of any one of them.

7.6.1 Specialist packages

There are a large number of these. CA Superproject, MS Project, Symantec Timeline and PMW for Windows are popular PC packages in the United Kingdom at the time of writing. There are others, and also complex packages designed to work on mainframe systems. Many packages can be networked allowing users in different locations to have access to project planning and reporting information. This is of considerable benefit to large multinational organizations whose projects often cross national and geographical boundaries.

7.6.2 Personal information managers

Many personal information managers (PIMs), either the electronic pocket book type or those designed to run on a personal computer, provide some basic scheduling support which can be used to manage projects.

7.6.3 A warning

Computer-based tools can become so fascinating that they can lead to a disease that is rife amongst certain project managers – replanititis. The main symptoms of this are that the manager spends so much time re-planning and updating the plan that they cease to spend any time actually keeping up with what is happening in the real world. This disease can be fatal.

7.7 Other tools

There are other tools that spring to mind but do not fit happily in any of the other sections of this chapter: flow charts and spreadsheets.

7.7.1 Flow charts

Although more often used for designing process control flows or computer programs, flow charts can be pressed into service for small projects where they effectively provide a cut-down PERT documentation aid. They can be particularly useful for documenting the higher level activities.

7.7.2 Spreadsheets

Although most of the arithmetic required of a project manager can be achieved using pencil, paper and, preferably, a calculator, use of a PC-based spreadsheet will make life much easier. They can be used for financial and resource recording/forecasting and allow frequently performed calculations to be templated so that considerable time savings are possible when faced with routine progress reporting, etc.

7.7.3 Prototyping

Another tool that can be adopted is prototyping. Here the idea is to test technology, the project management approach, or other variable on the basis of a small-scale trial to verify that the solution used is the right one and that the estimates that have been made can be justified. This is very useful where a large-scale investment has to be made on the basis of untried and untested estimates. Effectively running a small prototype project is a risk control exercise where the risk assessment of running the whole project is unacceptable without further information that can only be obtained from running the project as a pilot.

7.8 Project management methodologies

Now that we have covered the basic tools that are likely to be encountered when managing projects it is worth paying a passing mention to formal methodologies. Because organizations often have a wide range of projects going on, varying in size, importance, urgency, etc., they have found it necessary to standardize the approach they take. This has led to the development of many formal project management/development methodologies (e.g. the UK Government PRINCE system). These methodologies provide a framework for the documentation, control and management of projects within a particular environment. Typically they will define which documents have to be produced where and when (e.g. project initiation document, PID), who projects have to report to (e.g. project control boards, PCBs) and what tools are expected to be used, etc. These will be different for different organizations and projects and some sit more comfortably with particular types of projects than others. However, the reader will find that they almost all require the use of tools such as those described in this chapter and an understanding of what has been presented here should make the comprehension of one of these methodologies somewhat easier.

7.9 Methodologies: an example – PRINCE

The PRINCE methodology is built around a formal life cycle that has associated products with each stage in the life cycle. It is principally associated with the development of computer-based systems. However, it is generally applicable to any project and is in use in the commercial, government and business arenas. This subsection provides a brief overview only to give the reader a flavour of what to expect in a formal methodology. The idea is not to act as a PRINCE primer but to scope out what to expect from a methodology. Those who are familiar with PRINCE will readily appreciate that this constraint has been applied.

PRINCE is based on certain fundamental concepts:

- separating management from technical tasks;
- defining an organizational structure that encourages effective management and includes representatives of those who will use the end result of the project;
- identification of the best set of activities needed to deliver the project from analysis of the products that need to be produced;
- using control mechanisms to rapidly identify deviations from plan;
- detailed integration of quality management into the project from the start.

Note: The above are not the formal PRINCE definitions but have been simplified to make them more readily understood by the lay reader.

Within PRINCE a project is considered to be a set of **activities** whose completion results in a **product** (or products). The completion of all the activities results in a set of products which comprise the final deliverable to the client on whose behalf the project is undertaken.

Within PRINCE it is usual to sub-divide products into different types. A typical sub-division is described below.

- **Management products**: those products produced by management activities such as plans, progress reports, organization charts, project statements, etc.
- **Quality products**: those produced by quality management activities such as error reports, review meetings, audits, etc.
- **Technical products**: those produced as a result of technical work such as design specifications, computer programs, project specific tools, finished product, etc.

PRINCE is designed to promote the management activities which produce the technical products that conform to the required quality level. In other words the point of PRINCE is to provide the framework that enables people to manage the production of what is needed to fulfil the requirements of a project whilst making sure that it is done to a satisfactory quality.

In order to do this PRINCE uses three basic components: project organization, project planning and project control.

7.9.1 Project organization

Key to the philosophy of PRINCE are three organizational elements – a project control board (PCB), a project assurance team (PAT) and the project manager (or management team for large projects). These are there to exercise management and control at three levels: senior management, those who will use the project deliverables (customers) and those who perform the project work. Figure 7.10 shows how they work together and shows the feedback loop that exists to provide overall control of the project.

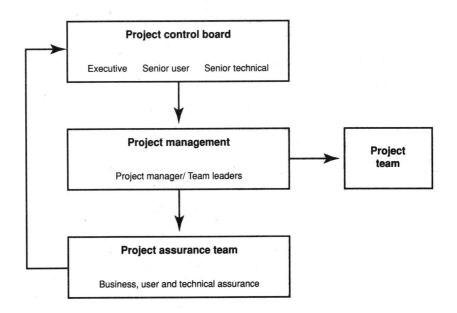

Figure 7.10 PRINCE components

Project control board (PCB)	The top level is the PCB which provides the senior management for the project. There are three roles that the PCB provides:

- the executive function which is responsible for the overall business of the sponsoring organization – typically the organization that foots the bill for the project team;
- the senior user (customer) representing the interests of those who will use the end product;
- the senior technical (implementor) who represents the people that make the products and deliverables.

These may be just three people, or a greater number where there is an overlap of responsibilities or the complexity of a project is such that no one person can represent the function in its entirety. The members of the PCB provide the top level of control, management and direction. They have the ultimate ownership for a project.

Project management

This is where the project manager fits in. He or she is responsible for day-to-day running of the project. The project manager will have freedom to operate within certain limits set by the PCB. In larger projects the project manager may have team leaders or other sub-project managers to help with the work. In PRINCE these are called stage managers.

Project managers are responsible for three things:

- achieving objectives with the most efficient use of resources;
- ensuring that products are produced that meet quality requirements and are on time and to budget;
- ensuring that all management and technical activities are completed.

Project assurance team (PAT)

The final component of the PRINCE organization is the PAT. This team is there to represent all groups at working level. Again is has three distinct roles: business, user and technical assurance. It exists mainly to support the project manager (or team). It is there to:

- monitor actual progresses against that originally planned;
- ensure that controls are properly administered;
- produce plans;
- monitor the project from the point of view of their individual speciality: business, user, technical.

7.9.2 Project planning

There will be a number of plans required within a PRINCE environment. Typical of these would be Technical Plans, Resource Plans, and Exception Plans.

- **Technical plans**: include the scheduling of technical activities that are needed to deliver the project deliverables including any related quality activities.
- **Resource plans**: show how much resource by type, time, support facilities required (e.g. office space), cost per unit time and total cost, etc.
- **Exception plans**: indicate the cause of significant deviations from plan together with corrective actions (see also contingency).

To allow for the scale of projects (i.e. large, medium, small) PRINCE also includes the facility to have a hierarchy of plans – project, stage and detail –

which are used by project managers, team leaders and individual team members respectively. A hierarchy of approval (PCB, project manager, team leader) goes with them to complete the loop. The idea is to provide the optimum level of detail at each level to allow the work to be completed and managed effectively.

7.9.3 Project control

There are many aspects of a project that can be chosen to control it. Three common choices for PRINCE are progress, change and quality. To do this control points are defined to check on relevant management, technical and quality issues. Essentially control points depend upon having detail specification of project products (deliverables), the ability to compare actual progress with project plans, having documentation of all problems and corrective actions, monitoring quality of deliverables, preventing unauthorized changes to the project, etc.

Progress control

This consists of checking that project deliverables (products) are being produced when they are supposed to be and that work is proceeding in line with the project plans. In addition it includes recording any problems that are detected and what actions are being taken to correct them.

Change control

This means having a complete set of procedures in place that ensure that all changes needed to cope with a changing world can be re-planned for. The key point is that a change cannot take place in an uncontrolled manner.

Quality control

The goal of quality control is to ensure that all products are complete, meet required specifications, meet relevant standards (e.g. safety standards) and are fit for the purpose for which they are intended. In many companies there will be complete quality procedures in place. Indeed, it is unlikely that any organization operating PRINCE, or a similar system, will not have such standards.

7.9.4 PRINCE summary

This subsection provides a flavour only of what a formal project methodology is like, for example no mention has been made of related documentation such as PID (project initiation document). The manuals for PRINCE run into hundreds of pages and it is quite normal for PRINCE training courses to last days or weeks depending of the level of detail understanding required. Such methodologies are not really appropriate for small projects; the overhead is too great. However, taking the basic principles and applying them as appropriate for your project can be very helpful. You may well come across PRINCE, or similar systems, in your working life and it is useful to understand that behind all the apparent complexity there is usually a core of good practice that can be applied generally. Do not let the jargon put you off.

7.10 Summary

There are many techniques, methodologies and tools available to support the project manager and their use is often determined by external factors such as the needs of the customer, the organization undertaking the project, government rules, etc. However, whatever the method the basic principles remain the same.

7.11 Exercises

7.11.1 General

Why are project management tools useful? What features would you expect to find in a project management tool? How might a computer/network based system offer additional benefits?

7.11.2 Gantt

Make a Gantt chart for a project to move a small business from one office to another. What are the advantages of using Gantt charts?

7.11.3 WBS

Using the plans from Question 7.11.2 as a starting point produce a multi-level plan for moving a manufacturing business from one site to another. The business employs about 200 people and has warehousing, engineering, transport and office facilities. These must all move during the same weekend and be operational by 09:00 on the Monday.

7.11.4 Pert

Production

Make a PERT chart for decorating a room. Identify the activities down to the level of individuals who will perform each task.

PERT versus Gantt

Why might you use a Gantt chart for this work instead of the PERT chart?

7.11.5 CPA

Identification

For the PERT chart that you have generated for Question 7.11.4 establish the critical path. Establish the minimum time that the job can be done. Why should you expect to revisit this analysis as the project progresses?

Benefits

What action might you take as a result of identifying the CPA? Why is CPA important?

7.11.6 Project scheduling

For one of the project plans created for the exercise above, or a project you are involved in, schedule it to be completed in the minimum time. Now schedule it for the minimum use of resource. making your own assumption for the hourly cost of the staff working on the project, estimate the difference in cost between the two schedules. Are there any other costs, e.g. overtime/shift working that might affect the costs? If so make an allowance for them. Are there any other problems that might affect the comparison?

Having looked at scheduling in the two extremes of time and resource limited, now define constraints for resource-limited scheduling, such as no weekend working and no more than 5 hours overtime a week. Next try and schedule the project with the goal of getting tasks completed as quickly as possible without breaking the resource constraints.

People and projects 1 (the project manager)

You've got to lead and not drive, inspire and not dominate, cause respect and not fear, win support and not opposition. Anon.

8.1 Introduction

The project manager, unsurprisingly, has a pivotal role in the running of a project. In order to fulfil this he or she will need a wide range of skills and personal qualities. In this chapter an overview is provided of these skills and qualities in use within a typical project environment.

8.2 Roles and responsibility

The role of the project manager has a number of facets:

- managing the project team;
- selecting team members;
- defining project objectives and goals;
- managing risk;
- managing change;
- negotiating with the client and the host organizations;
- problem resolution;
- financial management and reporting;
- measuring progress.

In performing these roles project managers have to consider four generic areas:

- the customer who will receive the project's end result;
- the project team;
- the host organization;
- the project itself.

Consequently there is an additional role in balancing the interests of these customers with each other, including the project team, for the lifetime of the project.

From these roles come the responsibilities – simply to perform the roles!

However they can be summarized in one core responsibility – the delivery of the project itself.

8.3 Skills

More than anything else a project manager needs a well developed portfolio of personal skills if a successful outcome is to be achieved. For convenience these have been divided into four main headings: communication, delegation, leadership and negotiation. There is no significance in the order, they are all essential!

8.3.1 Communication The ability to communicate effectively is a necessity for anyone managing a project. Project managers have to communicate in writing, make presentations, talk on the phone, use e-mail, and produce reports. They have to explain what needs to be done and also listen to what issues/suggestions project staff have. In other words nearly everything they do requires keen communication skills.

Webster's New Collegiate Dictionary defines 'to communicate' as:
*To transmit information, thought or feeling so **that it is satisfactorily received and understood.***

In the basic communication cycle, these are the stages that occur:

1 The need or desire to communicate with someone else – thinking, feeling, planning internally, setting objectives (**aiming**).
2 The translation of internal thoughts and feelings into an external means of transmitting them as a coherent message (**encoding**).
3 The transmission of the message (spoken, pictorial, written, body language, inflection, tone of voice, timing, visibility – **transmitting**).
4 The reception of the message (how and why people listen – **receiving**).
5 The translation of the message to internal thoughts and feelings on the part of the receiver (**decoding**).
6 The need or desire to respond to the message that has been sent. Thinking, feeling, planning internally, setting objectives (**responding**).

Figure 8.1 shows the communications cycle. There is one cardinal rule to remember for successful communication:

The meaning of the message is the responsibility of the sender and not the receiver.

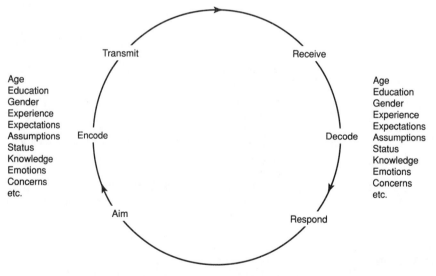

Figure 8.1 The communication cycle

The main points that we need to consider when we are communicating are:

Have I thought about how the receiver is going to understand what I am saying? Is the receiver ready to receive what I am about to say? How can I make my message clear? What do I want the receiver to do with my message?

1 Aiming checklist

- What do I want to communicate?
- Why do I want to communicate this?
- Who am I communicating with?
- What do I want the receiver to do with this information?
- What would make the receiver interested in my communication?
- What is the best way to communicate this?
- Have I prioritized my information?
- How much information should I give verbally or in writing?
- Will I need charts, pictures or diagrams?

2 Encoding checklist

- What language should I use?
- What does the receiver already know about what I am saying?
- Do we have a shared basis of knowledge?
- Do we have a shared basis of experience?
- What am I assuming about the receiver and are these assumptions valid?
- What might the receiver be assuming about me that would hinder effective communication?

3 Transmission checklist

- Is this the right time to communicate this?
- Can the receiver see/hear/read what I want to communicate?
- Will there be any distractions that will make communication difficult?
- Am I going at the right speed?
- Can I add anything to the words I use that will make my meaning clearer?
- How can I check that I am being received?
- Is what I am saying/writing/showing congruent with the way I'm saying/writing/showing it?
- Is my body language, tone of voice, inflection, eye contact and gesture congruent with what I am saying?
- Do I need to summarize?

4 Receiving checklist

Here is a list of 'listening habits' that will make communication more effective:
- Try to listen all the way through without judging or reacting.
- Always ask for clarification of anything that you don't understand.
- Check that any assumptions that you have made are valid.
- Only interrupt when you are confused or need clarification.
- Show that you are listening – nods, 'um hms', eye contact all encourage the speaker to continue.
- Take notes if necessary (but not if it interrupts the flow – we usually write at least three times slower than we speak).
- Look for unspoken messages.
- Listen actively – not passively.

5 Decoding checklist

- Don't be afraid to ask for clarification.
- Ask for a glossary of terms where necessary.
- Compare your experiences with what you already know, but don't always trust this if the subject is completely new to you.

Communications summary

The sender is responsible for the meaning of the message.
For successful communication to occur it is not enough to think about what you are going to say and how you are going to say it. It is vital that you consider your

listener's needs and attitudes. The way you encode your thoughts into words or visuals should take into account the way the receiver will decode that information into their own thoughts. Transmission of all messages should be as painless as possible for the listener and the sender needs to make sure that what they are communicating and the way they are communicating this information are congruent. Good listening is hard, there is a lot going on inside a listener's head, so good listening habits are well worth trying to achieve. When decoding new information don't be afraid to ask for clarification or extra information. When responding to a communication the shoe is on the other foot and the receiver becomes the sender and is therefore responsible for the meaning of his or her messages.

8.3.2 Delegation

A principal skill of anyone running a project is delegation. So what is delegation? Some people think of it as dumping work on the next level down the organization, or having it dumped on them.

Webster's New Collegiate Dictionary defines delegation as 'the act of empowerment to act for another'.

This is a very good definition as its wording implies that you are not just loading your work onto other people but giving them the responsibility to act in their own right. Delegation should be seen as passing on work for which you will both have responsibility, not passing the buck.

Delegating work downwards is the traditional view of the process. Typically tasks are off-loaded from the manager to other, less experienced, employees – for example preparation of a spreadsheet for a monthly report. In the case of project managers the strong element of team working makes this more of a partnership. If delegation in this environment is to be a success it is essential that what is required is clearly communicated and that you make sure that the delegatee is provided with everything needed to complete the task successfully. This communication of what is required is vital to all successful delegation; any shortcomings in this area will rebound on you very heavily, so check their understanding and do not rely on just telling them in your own terms. The first

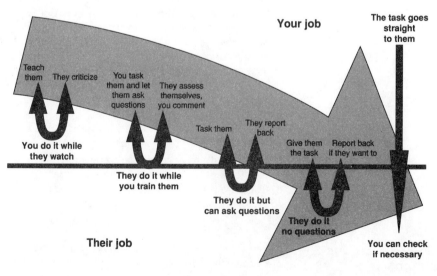

Figure 8.2 The process of delegation

time a particular task is delegated down to a less experienced member of staff you should expect to make a significant investment in teaching and advising. It is quite likely that the first time will involve you in almost as much work as doing it yourself. However, on subsequent occasions the amount of supervision should reduce and you will both reap the benefit.

Sideways delegation, to your peers, is becoming more commonplace. The flat structures of modern companies, with few layers of management, means that a large amount of co-operative working between staff at the same level has to take place. It is quite possible that the project manager may not be the most senior member of a team, technical consultants and other specialists may be senior to the manager. Typically you will be delegating something that you could do yourself to someone with similar levels of skill and experience.

An example from one of my customers concerned responding to a request for quotation from a prospective customer which had got lost in the system somewhere, i.e. the salesman had left it in his in tray for a fortnight and not told anyone about it. Consequently, what would have been a four week job had to be completed in two. Worse, another bid was in progress using up the resource that would normally have been scheduled for the job. The person responsible for producing the bid was able to delegate the task to one of his fellow managers who happened to have bid management skills and was able to get the job done. The job was delegated sideways to someone with a similar abilities. When delegating sideways you must be even more careful than usual to make sure that you do not present the work of others as your own.

An example of upwards delegation comes from a rigidly hierarchical company which has over ten layers of management. The problem was that the contractor concerned had been asked to document operating procedures for a computer application whose operation ran across both departmental and management boundaries. The system had been developed by the IT staff in one department at the behest of project sponsors whose authority did not extend outside of the department. However to operate effectively the system would have to be used by staff throughout the company. This meant that it was impossible to define operating procedures from within an isolated department. The solution involved writing a summary document which specified the reporting structures between the levels in the departments concerned, thus getting commitment to the project as a whole. Needless to say this generated all sorts of political fallout but it enabled the job, which was impossible as originally presented, to make progress. The upwards delegation consisted of supplying the management with a proposal to comment on so they could make the appropriate decisions. The essence of upwards delegation is that you are passing information or asking for policy decisions – you are not asking them to do the work for you.

The other side of delegation is defining what can and cannot be delegated. The following checklist should be considered whenever you think about delegating work.

- This is my task, I must do it.
- I ought to do this task but I can delegate it.
- It's possible for me to do it but it would be better if I delegated it.
- This must be delegated. I haven't the skill/time/resource to do it.

In general you should delegate tasks that are routine, well defined, necessary for day-to-day operation and achievable by the delagatee. You should not delegate such things as policy making, personnel matters such as evaluation, discipline, the act of delegation itself, resolution of disputes, and tasks specifically associated with your own status. Also remember that delegation is often a two-way process; by bringing a fresh light to a routine task the person to whom it is delegated may come up with a different or better way of doing it; you should evaluate this and take it on board and maybe change the way you would do that job.

Delegation is a valuable skill and works up and sideways as well as down within a project. Master it and you can arrange things so that you concentrate on doing what you are good at and, presumably, paid for. Get it wrong and the birds that come home to roost may be vultures. The key to getting it right is to make sure that all involved have a clear understanding of what is expected and when it needs to be done, in essence communication. It is a skill that can, and should, be cultivated. It is equally useful at all levels within an organization. Even the one man and a cat business involves delegation. For example, rodent control to the appropriate specialist.

8.3.3 Leadership

The leader must know that he knows, and must make it abundantly clear to those about him that he knows. Clarence B. Randall, *Making Good in Management* (1964)

All project teams need leaders, particularly at the start of a project. Wise project leaders are not concerned with their popularity at this point, more with the careful definition of the project, its goals, objectives and related tasks. Newly formed teams are not ready to perform until they understand what is expected of them both in tasks and standards. Failure to set clear objectives is one of the main reasons for poor performance.

People new to project management are usually good at actually performing tasks, but less skilful at setting clear goals and objectives for others. They often waste time telling their teams *how* to do their jobs rather than defining *what* the teams should be doing.

As with defining the overall project objectives (see Chapter 3) the acronym SMART (simple, measurable, achievable, realistic/resource, timetable), will allow you to evaluate objectives. To have your team paint the Forth Road Bridge blue by Tuesday is simple, it is measurable (it will have turned blue), it isn't achievable using current technology (you would need immense resource not just a few workers, so it isn't realistic), and the timetable is ludicrous. This example is not a serious one, but you get the point; nothing demotivates people faster than being made to work hard at something that can never be completed. Objectives may be difficult and challenging but they must be both possible and well defined.

Once the objectives have been set and checked, it is the project manager's responsibility to decide how they will be implemented. For example, the following questions are typical of those you should ask yourself. You will be able to think of more yourself along the same theme:

- What resource is need to get the work done? What are the external dependencies?
- Why do we need to do this? Why is it important?
- When do we need to start/complete the work? When do we need to tell other teams that we have completed it?
- How do I motivate the team to do it? How do we measure it? How will it affect other objectives?
- Where do I get the resources? Where will they sit?
- Who is going to help me? Who needs to know what actions I am taking? Who will benefit from the objective being achieved?

- Team objectives clearly set?
- Is it SMART?
- Individual goals defined?
- What, Why, When, How, Where and Who?

8.3.4 Negotiation

Negotiate: To confer (with another) for the purpose of arranging some matter by *mutual* agreement. (*Shorter Oxford Dictionary*).

Some people are natural negotiators and others find it embarrassing, but it is a fact of life that everything is negotiable. That said, negotiation is not a black art. The principles of the negotiation process have been well established. This section describes what may be negotiated, strategies that can be employed to meet different negotiation situations, and the negotiation cycle. The concepts are presented in a two-part case study that is based on a real life situation.

Case study: purchasing a computer – part 1

1 Introduction

Ask most people what there is to negotiate when they're buying a computer and they'll say, 'the price'. The more sophisticated might also mention bundled software, amount of memory and the screen size, but that is really only the beginning. We've come up with nearly 20 points that you could negotiate in a typical computer purchase. Figure 8.3 shows them in the form of a 'mind-map'; this starts from the concept of a deal and goes down different paths based on the major components of the specification, payment terms, software and support. Some of the individual points are elaborated upon below to give an idea of what to look for.

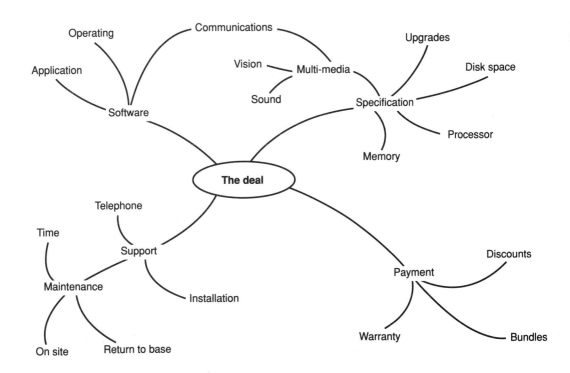

Figure 8.3 Mind map of negotiating deal

- **Specification:** How much disk storage space is there? How much semiconductor memory? How fast is the processor? What multi-media capabilities does it have? What is the cost increase/reduction for improving or reducing this specification? What scope for future expansion is there?
- **Payment:** What facilities are there for interest-free credit, reduction for payment by cash/cheque as opposed to credit card? Is payment by instalments available? What rental options are there?
- **Support:** How long is the machine guaranteed for? If it breaks will it be repaired on site or do you have to take it back to the shop? How quickly will they repair it? Can the warranty be extended for a reasonable price? Is a price reduction available for taking a reduced warranty? Is installation included or available if required? Are training courses available?
- **Software:** What applications software is available? What application software is included? Can the packages be changed for others more useful too you? At what cost?

To show that this is not all theoretical the authors offer the following example from personal experience in negotiating the purchase of a binding machine.

We wanted to buy a small wire-binding machine at a cost of not more than £200. We wanted to buy the wires and the covers from the same source and they had to be in particular colours. We wanted free delivery within three days for both the binding machine and the first batch of wires and covers, we wanted a year's free warranty and next-day delivery of wires and covers on an ad hoc basis. We expected to be buying regular, large supplies of these over the next few years. We also needed other office supplies – laser printer cartridges and ten reams of copier paper.

We did our homework and found that several stationery suppliers had just what we wanted at a variety of prices. The most expensive (and highest quality) machine was £20 more than we wanted to pay, but the supplier was reputable and could supply all that we wanted both at the time and in the future. We had also traded before and had found them to be very reliable.

The negotiation went like this:

'If you can drop the catalogue price by £30 we will order all our future binding supplies from you.' *(note that the initial demand was for more than we expected to get)*

'We'll go down £10 but no further.'

'Can you deliver it by next Thursday?'

'Yes, and we can deliver the covers and the wires at the same time.'

'Free delivery?' *(they usually charge £5 for delivery)*

'Not usually.'

'We need six sets of covers and two boxes of wires. If you throw in two sets of binder covers free I'll order my laser printer cartridges from you.' *(covers are worth £15)*

'OK is there anything else you need?'

'We might need some copier paper – are you doing any deals on that?'

'We've an offer on 100 gsm paper next week, 20 per cent off each ream.' *(worth £1 per ream)*

'If you give me the paper at the offer price you can deliver it next week with the binder.'

'OK'

'What deal are you doing on the laser cartridges?'

'The usual price, £60.'

'If you knock off 10 per cent on the cartridges I'll order two instead of one.' *(a saving of £12)*

'OK but you need to take three to get that discount.'
'What about the warranty on the binder?'
'Six months'
'If you up that to a year I'll put the order in now.'
'It's a manufacturer's warranty, we can't change it.'
'OK. What about future supplies of wires and covers – can you guarantee next-day delivery of these, bearing in mind that we'll be buying large quantities over the next year?
'We can do that.'
'This is a big order, if you can take another £5 off the binder we have a seal.'
'Done.'
'So just to recap, the binder at a discount of £15, 10 reams of paper at the offer price of £1 off per ream, three laser cartridges at a discount of 10 per cent, six packets of covers with two of these free, two boxes of wires, all delivered by next Thursday, and you will guarantee next-day delivery of covers and wires as we need them...'

There were a couple of other small points arising from the deal which were also sorted out easily but the general idea is clear. Admittedly this involved the salesman and ourselves in more work than just saying 'yes' to the original deal and it certainly made the salesman earn the commission, but in the end everyone got what they wanted. This type of negotiation is referred to as 'changing the package'. The overall value of the deal remains much the same, it is the components included that change.

3 Summary

So when you next come to negotiate something you should first define what it is you actually want; this is not only in terms of price, there are many other points to consider. This may not make you flavour of the day with the other party to the negotiation, but it should end up with everyone getting a better deal. In part two of the case study I will cover the how of negotiation and the techniques you can use once you've established what it is that can be negotiated.

Discuss what the negotiable factors are when buying a catering business. Do the same for selling a dry cleaning and shoe repair store. What are the common elements to both negotiations?

Case study: purchasing a computer – part 2

1 Introduction

First, a quick recap of Part 1 of the case study. Before you start any negotiation you should determine what it is that you are going to negotiate. In the case of the personal computer 20 different points were identified, it wasn't limited to the price! These points fell into the categories of software, support, specification and payment terms. These were further analysed to determine such items as disk space, memory, applications software, maintenance and telephone support.

2 Negotiation strategies

The first thing to do is choose the strategy to use. There are five main options to consider: win/lose, put it off, look at both sides, co-operate and solve the problem.

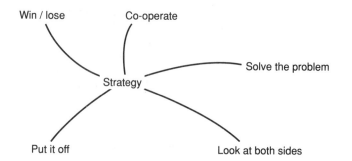

Figure 8.4 Mind map of negotiation strategies

- **Win/lose:** This is the adversarial method where you are negotiating to get the best deal you possibly can without any consideration for the other person. This is sometimes a successful one-off strategy. However, it does not work in the long term and project managers are rarely in this situation. This should only be considered when dealing with absolute non-negotiables or when you don't want to work with the same supplier or customer in the future.
- **Put it off:** Here you simply put off the negotiation until a future date. Usually this does not help as you will probably have to complete the negotiation eventually and there is no guarantee that things will be any better for you. However, it may be useful if a little time is needed to sort something out or get additional information. When doing this it is vital to identify how long you can put off the decision without losing out altogether; experience shows that there is a limit to how long you can put off a particular decision. Exceed it at your peril.
- **Look at both sides:** Here the idea is to make a conscious effort to listen to both sides of the negotiation and summarize the key points to ensure you understand them. It is an essential part of any good negotiation strategy and is useful at any stage in a negotiation. The authors recommend that you repeat this exercise often during an extended negotiation where people's circumstances will have changed as time passes.
- **Co-operate:** In this strategy each party recognizes the other's situation and acknowledges respect for it. This is a first rate position for beginning any negotiation and is the recommended default strategy.
- **Solve the problem:** You work with another party to define a joint solution, e.g. to agree a contract. The result of such a strategy should be a 'win-win' result which will lay firm foundations for future ventures. However, to do this requires firm preparation where you and the other parties get together to discuss all the points, and time constraints may have to be overcome to make sure this can be achieved. It also requires that the other parties involved wish to adopt a similar strategy and this is by no means certain. Indeed, a separate negotiation my be required first to reach the point where this strategy can be employed. It has been found to work well where the sale is complicated because of unusual customer requirements and where working within a team or consortium was necessary to win the business.

For a project manager the most useful are co-operate, look at both sides and solve the problem. The adoption of these strategies should enable you to get both a good deal and protect the long term interests of the project. Occasionally the put-it-off strategy can be of use in buying time and the solve-the-problem approach will be needed with suppliers. However, you should use win/lose at your peril, unless you are about to retire or don't want to manage any more projects for that customer!

Discuss what might be the best strategy to use in the following situations: re-negotiating the deadline for an interim project milestone that won't affect the ultimate project end date, obtaining additional staff resource from the departmental manager, getting a small change in specification agreed that will make the project much easier to complete to time.

3 The negotiation cycle

Once the strategy has been decided you can then get going on the actual negotiation. There is a simple five-step life cycle that can be applied to negotiation: plan, explore, offer, barter, close. Figure 8.5 shows this negotiation cycle.

Figure 8.5 The negotiation cycle

Plan Identify what it is you want and then prioritize as high, medium and low priorities. The high-priority items are the things that you really must have, such as an absolute latest delivery date, a maximum price, minimum specification, etc. This is the bottom line below which you cannot go. The medium-priority items are those that you would prefer to have but can survive without, possibly phased delivery and payment, extended warranty terms. The low-priority items are those which you might like but are certainly not worth risking losing a must-have for. Examples include having the equipment painted in a particular colour, intellectual property rights for re-sale.

At this stage you should also establish who you are negotiating with. In the case of third parties this is complicated by the fact that there may be an intermediary between you and the client. You may be negotiating with the intermediary as well as the company for whom you're to work, so you should try and define which parts of the deal affect which parties most. Typically the third party is concerned with margin and cash flow rather than your customer. You may be dealing with the people who wish to use the equipment but you have to get the order from a central purchasing department. The role of the people that you negotiate with will have an effect on how they negotiate. This brings us to the concept of decision makers and influencers.

- **Decision makers:** These are the people that actually make the decision about the outcome of the negotiation, effectively the people who put their names on the cheque.
- **Influencers:** These are the people who are involved in making the decision but do not take the responsibility for it. Typically they are advisors, technical specialists, legal experts and so forth.

It is important to establish that the person you are dealing with is the person that makes the decisions. For example, you may be having regular meetings with the people who will use the product you are selling once it has been purchased.

However, it may be the finance manager who has to approve the spend. In this case you will be dealing with the users of the systems as intermediaries, who will have the role of influencers but are not the decision maker.

How would you deal differently with decision makers and influencers? Which have you come into contact more often and why do you think this is the case? Have you any recent examples where you have come across influencers? How did you deal with them?

Explore   It is all too easy to miss this stage out and jump straight into the negotiations from the word go. This is a mistake, you will probably miss vital information for one thing but also, by failing to get some sort of rapport going with the other person, increase the risk of misunderstanding their meaning. Once such misunderstandings are made it is difficult to recover as your entire strategy will have been built on a falsehood.

When obtaining information you should use 'open questions'. Essentially this involves asking questions for which there is not a yes/no answer, encouraging the person to talk more freely and hence tell you what they think. You will often get pointers to further questions you hadn't thought of. An example of an open question is 'What are the main problems that you get from your existing computer system?' However, once you have got all the information you think you need you should always summarize what you have understood and gain agreement from the interviewee. This ensures that you are both negotiating about the same thing.

Offer   This is where the negotiation begins in earnest. Both parties will make their starting position clear: yours might be a monthly payment of £50 per month, paid quarterly in arrears, on site support and a price review after 12 months; theirs might be £70 per month, monthly payments in advance, fixed for 18 months with return-to-base support at your expense. It is important that you leave yourself room to manoeuvre, if your bottom line was £50 per month then you should have not made it your opening bid. Similarly you don't want to show all your bargaining counters up front, you need to keep them in reserve so you can make additional offers at a later stage. You can introduce them using the 'If ... then' technique (see below), where you make acceptance of one point conditional upon accepting another.

Barter   The nitty-gritty part of the negotiation and how you handle matters here will profoundly effect the outcome of the process. The key point here is never to give anything away without getting something back in return.

For example, the supplier may say that they can only supply for £60 per month when you were asking for £50. Don't just say 'yes', say 'yes, but I want a review after three months'. This brings us neatly to the next point; whenever you are bargaining make any changes conditional, 'If you ... then I'. For example, 'If you want me to pay £60 per month then I want on-site maintenance support instead of return-to-base'. A useful ploy is to link issues when bargaining. You can then play off one factor against another. Typically you might link a demand for payment in advance with free delivery. As this can start to get complicated, even with a simple supply contract, you must take notes as you go along so that you know where you are. And never forget the bottom line that you identified up front, you must never go below this – better no deal than a bad, or potentially ruinous, deal.

Close   The end. You have agreed a deal and defined what the terms and conditions are going to be. As stated in 'Explore' it is vital that all involved are sure that they have the same understanding as to what has been agreed. It is essential that this is written down and that what is written is agreed as binding. Whilst this is being done it is a good idea to reinforce the benefits that you are all getting from the deal and be prepared to be firm should it seem that negotiations are about to restart.

4 Negotiation summary

To summarize, there is a simple life cycle, Figure 8.5, that can be applied to a negotiation, use it and you should significantly improve the chances of a good result. Time and effort put in before you start negotiation will pay significant dividends. Remember that there is more to consider than simple price; there are many factors that don't cost money but significantly affect the quality of the deal struck. You may not wish to, or need to, negotiate every possible option but, the golden rule is - if you don't ask you don't get.

8.4 Summary

This chapter introduces the basic skills that the project manager will need in order to fulfil the roles and responsibilities that are required to manage the activities described in Chapters 3 to 6 of this book. The key aspects of these skills are communication, delegation, negotiation and leadership – and they are all dependent on the ability to communicate. In addition the project manager will need skills associated with the workings of the team itself, dealing with conflicts, external suppliers, etc., and these are covered in Chapters 9, 10, 11 and 12.

8.5 Exercises

Below is a list of the phases and their sub-stages in the project management cycle:

8.5.1 Communication

Definition phase

- Project statement
- Project objectives
- Project management discussion
- Work breakdown structure
- Resource requirements
- Risk assessment.

Planning phase

- Project planning
- Problem analysis
- Contingency and risk analysis
- Contingency planning
- Opportunity analysis
- Resource manager scheduling.

Implementation phase

- Project monitoring and control
- Project modification
- Managing change

- Performance analysis
- Project end.

By each phase and its sub-stages, note down the different types of communication needed for each. You will find that there is often the need for more than one type of communication during each phase and stage.

Types of communication:

a) Written (in the project file)   b) Group meetings   c) Individual meetings (one on one)

d) Formal letter/report   e) Informal get together   f) Briefing document

g) Formal presentation   h) Brainstorming session   i) On-site chat

j) Motivational session   k) Memo   l) Up-date session

8.5.2 Delegation

Why is delegation such an important skill for a project manager? Give at least three reasons.

What should a project manager try to delegate and what should she/he never delegate?

8.5.3 Leadership

At the start of a project it is particularly important for the leader to do one particular thing. What is it?

8.5.4 Negotiation

What are the five stages in a negotiation?

No one can whistle a symphony. It takes an orchestra to play it. Halford E. Luccock

9.1 Introduction

Team working is at the heart of all projects, after all by definition a project requires a project team to implement it. People often behave in a characteristic way when working in a group which is quite different to the way they work individually. There are many more factors to consider when working with others; for instance, your status within the project team may be different to your status in your normal job, your speed of working or set of priorities may be different to other members of the team and this may cause problems for each of you. You may be located in other people's space or in unfamiliar territory, you may even have split loyalties where it is difficult to align your responsibilities as a project team member with your day-to-day job responsibilities. On top of all this you may well be asked to work with people you have never met before and need to get to know before you can work well with them.

Consequently, this whole chapter is dedicated to team working and how to do it more effectively. We have also included a section on running successful meetings, since this is one of the main activities where the main team or sub teams are likely to be interacting together.

9.2 Working in teams

The key elements to understanding team working rest in knowing the stages of team formation, establishing team norms, paying attention to team dynamics and an analysis of how successful teams work and what is likely to threaten this.

9.2.1 Team formation

When a group of people form a team, they go through a series of behaviours that help to mould the team into a working unit. These stages always occur when the team members are new to each other and the project. There are three basic stages that the team must go through before they can begin to perform.

Forming

When a group of strangers first come together they desperately need to know what they are there for. They have a head full of unanswered questions that concern them: 'Why am I here?' 'What are we expected to do?' 'How long is this going to take?' 'What are our objectives?'

This is the 'forming' stage in team development, and until every person knows what they are there for, both as individuals and as a group, they simply will not get down to any work. The project manager's main responsibility at this point is to ensure that clear objectives are set, talked through and agreed, both verbally and in writing.

Anything that helps to identify the team with the project is useful at this point. It may seem a small point, but very often a project team name can help with this process. Some of the most effective project teams we have worked with not only had a name but also a logo which identified everything that the team produced, they also had a slogan or mission statement that clearly stated what they were trying to achieve.

Lack of direction at this point is lethal. The forming stage is rather like the start of a relay race where every participant needs to know where the start and finish line is and what the rules are that control the race's smooth running. Imagine the chaos if this information wasn't given to all the participants before they started.

Storming

Now that the project's objectives and goals have been set the members of the team begin to ask another set of questions: 'Who is in charge here?' 'What is my status in the team?' 'Who else is in the team?'

This is the 'storming' stage in team development where each member begins to mark out their own position within the team. The project manager needs at this point to make sure that the team gets to know what each person is going to do, who reports to who and what is expected of each team member. People have a natural need to not only test out their position within the team, but also to tell the rest of the team something about themselves and their background. The project manager can help with this process by introducing each team member in turn to the group and telling the team why each person is involved with the project.

Often at this point there may be a challenge to the project leader from one or more members of the newly formed team. This may seem uncomfortable for the leader, but is an important testing of both the project leader's ability to control events, and the need for powerful personalities to make their mark on the proceedings. A wise project manager will handle any such challenge with diplomacy and firmness, bearing in mind that what the team needs at this point is strong leadership and direction, while understanding the reasons for the challenge.

Norming

The team is coming together at this point, but there is still one further stage that needs to take place. This is the 'norming' stage, where the team, often quite spontaneously, begins to produce a set of spoken and unspoken rules about the way they will work together. Some of these norms are quite specific. For instance: how often they will meet, how they will communicate with each other and the leader and how often. Other norms are more personal: things like how disclosive the team is (whether they share personal information), how formal or informal they will be, how they dress, how punctual they will be, how enthusiastic they are about their tasks and so on. These norms make the team feel comfortable and give the team a unique identity. The norms represent the face the team presents to the world. If any team member refuses to abide by these norms the team will often subtly edge the dissenting member out. Team norms may take a little time to develop (usually by the third or fourth team meeting they will be established) but they are an essential part of the team's smooth functioning.

9.2.2 Group norms discussion

What are the norms within your group of friends?
What about norms in other groups – for instance in banking, public transport or the arts?

9.2.3 The basic composition of successful teams

When we work with a team we have two functions. First we have a set of tasks to perform. These task skills and behaviours are usually why we have been included in the team in the first place. Expertise in areas like technology, selling, planning, accounting and construction and so on helps the team to fulfil the tasks that must be performed in order to satisfactorily complete the project. The project manager obviously will want the most competent and expert people within the project as he/she can possibly find. Indeed, when putting the project team together he/she will have defined the skills needed in the work breakdown structure phase of planning the project (see Chapter 3).

However, there is another important function of being a team member, and that is your *role* within the team. Your team role depends very much on your personality and although your team role may well help you and the rest of the team to fulfil your tasks successfully, it is mainly concerned with keeping the team healthy and united. Team roles are concerned with things like good leadership, team support, ideas generation, peace keeping, attention to detail, motivation and interaction with other teams.

If a project manager doesn't pay attention to the way the team functions, in other words keep the proper balance between the roles in the team, then even a team of absolute experts will not be as successful as a team of, perhaps less expert, but much more integrated individuals.

9.2.4 Individual team roles

The four essential team roles we will look at here are the leaders, the opponents, the supporters and the outsiders.

1 Leaders

In Chapter 8 we covered some of the qualities and actions needed to be a successful project leader, however there will be times when the project manager must relinquish his/her leadership role to another team member. Take the example of site management on a large construction project; here the project manager would not be expected to be the everyday controller of the site activities, he/she may not even have the required skills and knowledge for this job, so a site manager would be appointed by the project manager to look after the multiplicity of tasks that are needed at the site. To the site workers, the site manager is their leader, and it is to him/her that they will report, ask for decisions and take their problems. It is true that the site manager will report to the project manager within the hierarchy of the project itself, but it is poor policy for the project manager to interrupt the clear reporting structure between the site manager and his/her staff. To do so undermines the authority of the 'local' leader and leads to confusion over responsibilities. When the project manager does visit the site, his/her role is that of a motivator, strategic planner or observer, and not someone concerned with the day-to-day running of the site.

Even in smaller projects there are likely to be 'local' leaders who look after smaller teams and who report back to the project manager, and, just as with large projects, the lines of reporting and responsibility need to be clearly laid out, so the 'going over the bosses head' problems do not occur.

These 'local' leaders should be chosen not only for their ability to perform the tasks needed, but also for their ability to manage teams. A shy, introverted, ultra-cautious super-techie, who prefers to work alone and look after the minutest details may not be the best choice as a 'local' leader even though his/her ability to perform the necessary tasks is not in doubt.

So what are the qualities that make people successful leaders? An interesting piece of research was done in the 1990s by Coleman and Barrie. They interviewed 3000 workers and asked them 'What are the general qualities that you value most in a team leader or manager?' And these were the answers:

- Consistency
- Good listening skills

- Firmness
- Sense of humour
- Honesty
- Strength
- Decisiveness
- Fairness
- Communicativeness
- Supportiveness
- Being open to ideas.

2 Opponents

Where there are leaders there will inevitably be opponents. It's human nature, particularly if the leader's style is autocratic or particularly directive. These opponents may express their opposition to the leader openly, or may covertly work to undermine the leader's authority. This all sounds as if it might lead to considerable problems, and if handled badly may well do so. The fact is that healthy dissent should be welcomed in a team. Unconditional acceptance of a leader's ideas and decisions may seem a quick way of getting things done (and indeed in certain situations like army manoeuvres, or emergency procedures for instance, may be essential), but slavish obedience actually negates the real advantages of working as a team. These advantages are many. Team decisions are often of a higher quality than individual decisions, the array of differing skills and experience that individuals bring to a group enterprise will not only raise the quality of the finished product but will also result in better working methods. People work best when their input is valued and encouraged, so even if this input may take the form of disagreeing with the leader or challenging the way things are being done this input should be appreciated and discussed.

The project leader may well be skilled in many aspects of the project, but cannot possibly be expert in everything. It is particularly important to encourage healthy opposition at the planning stage of the project, when contingency planning and risk analysis is so important.

3 Supporters

These people keep the team machinery oiled and running smoothly. They are the group members who look after the social health of the team. They often personally prefer to work in a group and gain most satisfaction from activities where they are interacting with others. They encourage friendship between the team members, they support and maintain the team norms, they watch out for unfairness and victimization. They are willing to join in and help out where they are needed and they support the leader loyally. They are very useful indeed. There are, however, one or two dangers if a team is overburdened with supporters. These are that the supporters can be so concerned with the internal needs of the team that they may put the completion of tasks into second place, or they may be so willing to help other people out that they unwittingly neglect their own tasks. Flattering and comfortable though it may be for a project manager to have a loyal band of supporters, it is always worth keeping an eye on the actual progress of the project, the length of time taken up with meetings and socialization and the amount of unqualified obedience that occurs in any decision making processes.

4 Outsiders

All teams need outsiders, but it is also true to say that practically every team we've worked with has found the outsiders the most difficult to cope with. Outsiders take a cool, uninvolved view of what the team is up to. They may do this for many reasons. Perhaps they are genuine outsiders, brought in to add an external expert's knowledge to the team's efforts. Perhaps they have split loyalties because they are involved external groups which means they can see the impact of the your team's behaviours and tasks on other parts of the organization more clearly that you can. Perhaps they have a personality style which makes them more comfortable to step back from involvement and group activity. They may even be included within the team as an auditor of cost, quality or working practices. Indeed, new members brought into an established team very often take the role of outsider until they are integrated into the group.

To the rest of the group the outsiders seem to be faintly (or even overtly) critical and not particularly enthusiastic about the team's actions and goals. Quite naturally, enthusiastically involved team members who are fully committed to the project feel resentful of this unengaged view and may have a tendency to disregard any input from the outsider. This is a great pity, since it is the outsiders who give the team a sense of proportion.

A wise project manager will make the most of the outsiders in his/her team by asking for their observations and inputs. It is all too easy to become so involved in the successful working of your project that you lose sight of how this fits in with the rest of the organization.

9.2.5 Factors affecting team performance

These are the critical factors that affect how your project team works. When managing a project team you need to consider these factors since they will all have an impact on the successful outcomes of the project.

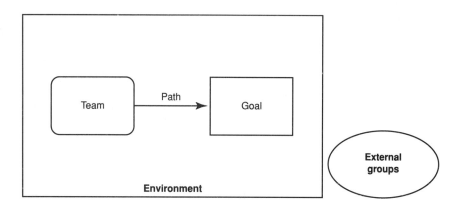

Figure 9.1 Factors affecting team performance

1 Team

The people who work together in the project team. Apart from the team roles discussed in Section 9.2.3, the factors that influence the team are:

- **Size.** If the team is large there will be a definite need to break it down into sub-teams with their own leaders. Reporting structures and escalation procedures must be carefully defined. If the team is small (less than four) then members may need to double up on their team roles to ensure that there is a healthy mix of leaders, opponents, supporters and outsiders.
- **Maturity.** Young teams (teams that have never worked together before) need fairly directive leadership where the project manager makes certain that everyone is told what is expected of them, the time scales, the quality standards and the costs involved. Tasking must be impeccable with no room for misunder-

standing. As the team works together and becomes more mature it will need less tasking from the project manager and more encouragement and motivation. As the team becomes mature the project manager should delegate as much as possible to allow the team to develop. This does not mean that the project manager in any way loses control over the overall project, more that the team takes on more and more responsibility for their own actions. The project manager must still know what is going on, but should not need to personally oversee every facet of the project.

- **Personalities.** Every team will be composed of different personalities. This is one of the benefits of team working. On the other hand, conflict may arise because of the different ways that each personality goes about prioritizing and performing the tasks set for them. The project manager needs to be aware of how each team member likes to work: factors such as speed of working, how cautious or adventurous people are, whether they like to work alone or in a group, whether they are concerned with detail and precision or more concerned with ideas and experimentation, whether they like to lead or follow, whether they become impatient with long drawn out tasks or prefer systematic, methodical work. The project manager needs to observe his/her team members carefully and try to allocate tasks and parcels of work in such a way as to maximize the potential of each personality.

For example, we once worked with a small but very mixed team on a project to run a conference for the senior management of a large financial institution. There were only five members in the project group, one was brilliant at ideas and starting things off (1), but less effective when having to finish tasks that had to be done in a meticulous way, another team member (2) was quiet, shy, dedicated, an absolute perfectionist who was very cautious about making decisions. Of the other three members, one was a gregarious and outgoing personality who was happiest when developing ideas and working in a group (3), another was a tough, businesslike woman who liked to have everything under control and was particularly good at negotiations (4) and the final member was a complete networker with a huge range of contacts who was surprisingly patient when solving problems (5).

Amongst our project tasks we needed to:

a) Compile a complete list of all attendees and speakers with their contact addresses, telephone numbers and e-mail numbers.
b) Persuade two or three members of the management team to run a breakout session during the conference.
c) Book a hotel for the conference venue which would fulfil all our needs.
d) Brief a design company on the staging and documentation for the conference.
e) Set up a system to record all conference expenditure during the life of the project.
f) Work with the management team to identify what they wanted to cover on the conference.
g) Prepare a work schedule for the entire project and teach the rest of the project team to use it.
h) Find and then brief a production company to take care of the lighting a sound for the conference.

Which task would you have allocated to which people?

2 Goal

We have covered this in depth in Chapters 2 and 3; however, it never hurts to repeat an absolute truth:
The most common reason for project failure is unclear or inexact goaling and objective setting.

3 Path

This refers to how the goal is to be achieved. Obviously, if care is taken at the project definition and planning stage the path to the goal should be clear. There are several other factors that need to be considered about the path to the goal.

How long will the project take? Some projects are quickly completed and the pace and enthusiasm generated by a new undertaking does not dissipate. However some projects may take years to complete (think about some of the projects in the American Space Program which took three or more years). Longer projects bring their own problems. How do you keep the enthusiasm and pace going? (Regular team meetings, celebrations of short-term successes, breaking long-term objectives into timely chunks.) What will happen if people leave and others join the project group? (Expect the need for the form, storm, norm cycle to take place again.) Will people lose sight of the overall objectives? (Yes, unless these are regularly referred to and clarified.) Do you need milestones along the way to give the team something to aim for at regular intervals? (Yes.) Will people become complacent about quality standards or careless about safety regulations? (Certainly, unless these are regularly checked and updated and the risks re-analysed at regular intervals.)

This is why we said that the project planning stage is merely a starting point and that plans must be continuously revisited and adapted to reflect the reality of working in a changing world.

4 Environment

This refers to the surroundings in which the team works. Not only the physical surroundings but the commercial, social and ethical environment in which the team performs. Continual attention needs to be paid to the effects this environment may have on the team's health, both psychologically and physically.

What external considerations might make the team work less productively? Factors such as company policy and the way it is administrated, pay scales, working conditions, team and individual status, supervisory practices, security and interpersonal relationships between the team and the rest of the company. These factors have been defined by Herzberg as 'hygiene factors' and if these are unsatisfactory this will cause dissatisfaction in the team. This is not to say that people will not work well in imperfect environments – many project teams work in terrible conditions of heat, cold, danger, isolation, poor pay, discomfort and uncertainty and still achieve their objectives. Danger to performance arises when not only are the hygiene factors unsatisfactory but there is also a lack of what Hertzberg called motivators (factors like recognition of a job well done, achievement of tasks, taking responsibility for yourself and other people, personal growth, advancement, pride in the work itself). In this situation the team is unlikely to perform well at all, being both demotivated and dissatisfied.

If conditions arise where the hygiene factors are poor, then the project manager should do everything possible to improve them, as well as keeping the internal motivation of the team at a high level.

5 External groups

These are outside groups which can affect the team, including those which have goals that conflict with the teams, those who have staff seconded to the team, or those competing for the same resources. In modern business, where staff numbers have been pared to the bone and people may have many, possibly time conflicting tasks to perform, this becomes a real problem. Where do individual loyalties lie? To the person's direct manager, to the project leader, to the project, to other groups within the company? The project manager needs to be aware of any conflicting time or priority pressures on his/her team members. In tightly run companies, this will mean co-operation with other managers and group leaders, careful scheduling and a contingency plan for key project personnel that takes account of possible absences or delays.

9.2.6 Communication within teams

Is the communication cycle any different when we work within teams or groups? Not really, we still need to aim, encode, transmit, receive, decode and respond just as effectively (see Chapter 8). However, there is a special factor that enters the equation when we work in project groups – timeliness. There is a crucial need for the project manager to be in possession of up-to-date information about the progress (or otherwise) of the project *at all times*. What is more, this information needs to be communicated as quickly and effectively as possible to *anyone* it affects. This necessitates established and reliable physical communication equipment such as e-mail, telephones, faxes, internal mail, teleconferencing, paper mail, computer networks and so on, with a clear set of associated procedures. The whole team should know how and when to contact their leaders, subordinates and co-workers and should be encouraged to do so – *particularly if things go wrong.* There is a human tendency to avoid being the bearer of bad news and to try to hide failures until they become so major that they escape all on their own. The attitude of the people managing the project and its associated tasks should encourage free reporting of faults and failures without fear. Hypercritical, judgmental and blaming attitudes work against the free flow of information. There are bound to be snags in any project; these are best handled when they are in their infancy and a stitch in time can save overspending, over-running and serious interruption of the project.

9.2.7 Groupthink

So here we are with a perfectly balanced project team, well integrated in terms of team roles, impeccably tasked and goaled. Everyone is performing effectively with cohesive norms and good leadership, communicating freely and fearlessly amongst themselves with all the hygiene and motivation factors at an optimum level. Even the project is on target and slightly under budget; what could possibly go wrong?

Groupthink, that's what.

It seems really unfair that this only affects cohesive and bonded teams. In the 1980s Irving Janis identified groupthink as a serious threat to effective decision making and risk analysis. What happens is that the group's psychological need for unanimity and consensus suffocates any dissent or analysis of alternative choices. Even expert input may be ignored if it goes against the majority verdict.

A horrible smugness pervades the team, any threats to the team are dismissed as not worth thinking about, silence is taken to mean consent, people actually appoint themselves as 'mind guards' and discourage any dissent or individual doubts. The pressure for the team to agree peacefully over everything is overwhelming, so much so that reality becomes uncomfortable. You can imagine what this does in the hurly burly of a project. Decisions become sloppy, risks are overlooked, the team settles comfortably into its own little world, and things begin to go wrong.

Curing groupthink is easy if it is in its early stages. Simply make sure that there is someone acting as a devil's advocate, and that rigorous examination of alternatives continues. The project manager needs to check that those taking the opponent or outsider roles are not being ignored and a healthy scepticism about 'everything going smoothly' should be fostered.

If groupthink is really advanced in a team, it probably won't be noticed by the team itself, and decline and failure of the project may well follow. Prevention is truly better than a cure in this case.

9.3 Meetings

The length of a meeting rises in direct proportion to the square of the number of people present. Eileen Shanahan.

Any project manager is going to spend a fair amount of time in meetings; projects often seem to revolve around them because they provide a convenient method for broadcasting and forming decisions. Experience shows that there are rather more bad meetings than we would like; however, there is something you can do about this.

9.3.1 Agenda

First of all have an agenda. Without one of these you stand no chance. It can be just scribble on the back of an envelope, but it is vital. However, before you can develop an agenda you need an objective for the meeting; if you can't find one, then this is the time to call a halt to the proceedings and cancel the meeting. Don't have a meeting unless you really need one. Once you know why you're having it you can decide who should be there. For example, at a technical review meeting you would expect to have the project manager, technical representatives and probably someone from the quality department. The goal is to only have people who are actively involved with meeting present; additional attendees only drag the proceedings out. Indeed, you may choose to have different people present for different items on the agenda bringing in specialists as needed. This saves the waste of having an expensive resource sitting in on a one-hour meeting just to cover an agenda item that lasts five minutes. Mind you, there may be political reasons why someone needs to be at a meeting even though they don't contribute directly – the project manager should make allowances for this as they consider fit.

9.3.2 Logistics

Logistics comes next. Find a suitable location for the meeting with sufficient table and chair space and appropriate facilities such as a whiteboard or an overhead projector as needed. Too many meetings fail because someone decided to hold it at their desk in an open plan office.

To ensure that all the participants can make it, give everyone a reasonable period of notice; a week is about right. This will considerably improve your chances of getting the people needed for the meeting there, or at least provide time to re-schedule for a more convenient time. It is pointless having a meeting with key staff missing. Make sure that people know when and where it is too; this may sound obvious but it is surprising how often people are left to guess for themselves. Furthermore people must be told what the agenda is so that they can prepare before the meeting rather than having to wing it on the day. It is pointless asking someone to describe a complex project plan at five minutes' notice; try and give them a couple of hours so they have plenty of time to panic about it!

9.3.3 Chairing meetings

The meeting itself. A good chair(person) is worth their weight in gold. The project manager can expect to take on this role for most of the internal project meetings and some of the external ones as well. This role includes ensuring that the agenda is followed, that debate is not allowed to get 'rat-holed' into in-depth technical issues when they are not relevant to the task in hand and that discussions aren't allowed to metamorphose into arguments, or even violence (it has happened!). In addition, the chair(person) must make sure that all decisions are summarized so that everyone present is clear what the consensus is. This leads onto the topic of minutes (see also Section 9.3.2); it is essential to record all decisions and actions for reference in the future. Experience shows us that people have remarkably different memories of the same meeting, particularly if they haven't done something that they were supposed to.

9.3.4 What next?

Lastly it is a good idea to end the meeting with a 'what next' session. This may only determine when the next meeting should be or it could determine a completely new agenda.

If you do all these things then you will be well on the way to having a productive and, if you are lucky, a short, meeting. If you are not running the meeting yourself then you can at least make sure that you ask for an agenda, establish what is expected of you, and prepare beforehand knowing when and where it is. A wise project manager will also encourage all the team members to adopt this approach.

9.3.5 Meetings Summarized

Key points:

- have an agenda;
- make sure people know when and where it is;
- what they need to do before the meeting;
- why they are invited;
- record actions and decisions;
- agree next steps;
- keep it relevant.

9.3.6 Minutes

Project progress meetings, business reviews and formal customer meetings have to be minuted. The reason for this is to make sure that there is a permanent record of what was agreed and what courses of action people undertook to carry out. This record can then be used to measure progress and ensure that there is a common understanding of what is to happen and what has happened.

The starting point for any set of minutes is that they should indicate who was at the meeting, where and when it was. Next they should be used to record any key facts and who supplied them, and the resolution of any debates. Note that it is usually unnecessary to record everything that was said or how decisions were reached. However, there will be occasions where one or more people at a meeting will wish to formally state their disagreement with a majority decision; in this case they may ask that their point of view be minuted to show that they were of a different opinion to the group.

The other key function of minutes is to record who has committed to do what, normally referred to as 'actions'. When recording actions in minutes it is normal to adopt some form of abbreviated notation to link the actions with the meeting and the individual(s) concerned. For example, an action taken at a meeting held on 12 August '96 for David Nickson to do something might be identified as 12/08/96-DN-1/1, the 1/1 showing that it was the first action given at the first meeting. This provides a valuable means of tracking progress against the actions, it also makes it visually clear which actions are outstanding and from how long ago. If you are having your tenth meeting and there is an outstanding action labelled 08/01/96-DN-2/1 then you know that there is a problem with this action and that it should be actively reviewed.

It is not always essential to incorporate the date in an action identifier – the meeting number may suffice and makes for shorter references. However, it can be an advantage to have the date there to make it readily apparent how much time has passed since the action was placed.

Minutes of the 4th new business marketing meeting

Meeting held at The Chequers, Oxfordshire
Date 21/09/96   Time 10:00 hours
Those present: Usha G, Nigel P, Kate A (Chairperson), Philip A, David A (Secretary).
Apologies for absence: Sid, Pat.

1 Minutes of last meeting
These were accepted as being a true and accurate record of the previous meeting and were duly signed by the secretary.

2 Matters arising
There were none.

3 Review of actions
re: UG-3/1
UG reported that the purchase of the Grange Farm agricultural units had been completed and that architects had been asked to tender for the work of planning the new business units. Action completed. KA was asked to draw up selection criteria for choosing the architects.
Action KA-4/1

4 New business
NP suggested that it would be necessary to make sure that local feelings were taken into account when promoting the new business units. He was willing to investigate the sponsorship of a children's playground in the local village.
Action NP-4/2

5 Any other business
DA asked that the access roads for the development be designed so that tractors could still use them for reaching fields under cultivation adjacent to the new business units. This was agreed and will be forwarded to the architects once commissioned.
Action UG-4/3

6 Next meeting
The next meeting was scheduled to be held at 12:00 on the 4th November '96, in the Blue Boar Oxfordshire.

The agenda to be unchanged.

It is very important to have a formal agenda for any meeting which is to be minuted. The agenda will provide the structure for the minutes. This is in addition to the other benefits that arise from having meeting agendas in terms of control and direction of the meeting.

Why is it important that minutes are agreed at the start of the next meeting? Discuss the statement 'minute taking is power'.

9.4 Summary

Team working is a major factor in any project. Good teams don't just happen by accident. The project manager needs to consider the factors that affect good team working, not only during the implementation phase of the project, but also during the planning phase. Teams need constant monitoring, the team roles of leaders, opponents, supporters and outsiders need balancing and developing since during the life cycle of a project team these will change as the team becomes more mature and used to working together. There are many factors that influence the health of a team; these too need to be monitored and catered for, perhaps necessitating re-planning and re-prioritizing during implementation. Environmental factors and the presence of external teams can seriously impede good team practices and need to be considered as part of project management activities. Lastly beware of groupthink – at the first sign of complacency or softness take remedial action, or all your good work will have been in vain.

9.5 Exercises

9.5.1 Team formation

What are the three stages in team formation that need to take place before the team can perform well? What happens during each stage?

9.5.2 Team Roles

What are the four team roles needed for a healthy team?

9.5.3 Groupthink

Why is groupthink so dangerous to successful teams?

9.5.4 Meetings

List as many key points as you can that would lead to a successful meeting.

10   People and projects 3 (third-party suppliers)

If you want good service, serve yourself. Spanish proverb

10.1 Introduction

In Chapter 5 the topic of dependencies was covered; these dependencies include those specific to third party suppliers. However, dealing with third parties can be a significant part of a project manager's job, so this chapter has been given over to this and the skills required in doing this effectively.

10.2 Who is a third party?

This apparently simple question has no simple answers. At first sight you might say that anyone in a different company or organization to the one the project team operates in is a third party. For example, for someone implementing a new electronic mail system within a company it might be the computer supplier, a cabling contractor, builders, software suppliers and consultants who are the third parties. However, the real definition needs to include anyone outside the project team, *irrespective of who they work for.* Your immediate boss can be considered as a third party if not an integral part of the team.

A third party is anyone involved with a project who is not an integral part of the team. Within an organization this typically includes those who control the budget, the provision of staff resource, internal services, building services, etc. These all need to be viewed as external suppliers and treated with the same caution as those sub-contractors/suppliers who are external to the project team's organization.

10.3 Key points for third-party suppliers

The following points apply to all third-party suppliers:

- outside direct control;
- you are their customer;
- have own goals/objectives;
- have own ways of working;
- know things you don't;
- don't know things you do.

To expand on these…

10.3.1 Outside direct control

This is the most obvious aspect of a third-party supplier. Their staff do not report to you or your team directly. Consequently no-one in the project team is in a position to change the service that is being provided to the customer without going through an intermediary. This requires that a strong reporting plan is put in place.

Here is an example of a project where a customer (The Mighty Stores Group Ltd) needed to install new tills in each of its high street stores (150 in all). These new tills were designed and made by Snapshut Tills plc. The finished tills were then shipped to each high street outlet where they were installed by Shiftem Installations Ltd.

Figure 10.1 shows the way they were organized:

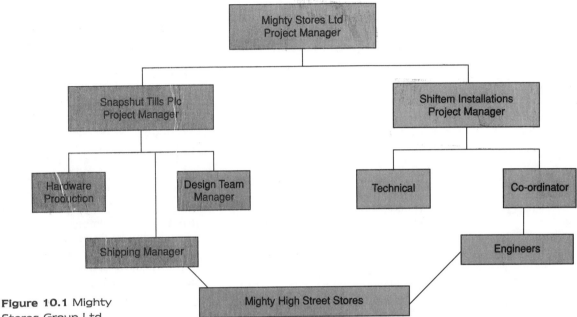

Figure 10.1 Mighty Stores Group Ltd

This looks quite simple, doesn't it? If there was a problem with the hardware production, this would be communicated to the Snapshut Tills project manager, who might or might not need to report this to the Mighty Stores project manager. Or if one of the engineers did not turn up, this would be reported to the Shiftem Installations co-ordinator, who might or might not need to report this to the Shiftem project manager who might or might not report this to the Mighty Stores project manager.

But what happens where there is a problem that involves both the Snapshut Tills team *and* the Shiftem Installations team?

In fact this was exactly what happened. On the first day of the installation programme, the stores were sent the wrong hardware by Snapshut Tills. The engineers who were on site waiting for the kit, immediately contacted their co-ordinator who then had several options:

(a) He could contact the Snapshut Tills shipping manager and sort out the problem with him directly.
(b) He could contact the Snapshut Tills project manager, who would then contact the Snapshut Tills shipping manager who would then sort out the problem.
(c) He could contact his (Shiftem Installations) project manager, who could contact the Snapshut project manager, who would contact his shipping manager who would sort out the problem.

Well this could go on an on, with each person reporting up the chain to the main Mighty Stores project manager who would then cascade the problem back down to the Snapshut shipping manager.

And that would be ridiculous, wasting so much time that the problem would become even bigger.

So what is needed is careful thought in the planning and implementation phases about how problems can be solved quickly and effectively without involving elaborate escalation procedures. A set of procedures for fixing non-serious on-site problems needs to be thought out and direct communication lines between the concerned groups set up.

The ideal solution to the wrong kit problem was (a), where the co-ordinator directly contacted the shipping manager and solved the problem quickly with the least waste of time. This problem would only have needed escalating if it happened over and over again and seriously impacted the time or cost scales of the project.

All this said, it is also important to keep a record of problems that have occurred and include them in the on-going project reports given to the overall project manager. There may be a pattern there which the individual groups could not see, but which can be spotted by the helicopter view of the chief project manager.

A set of guidelines about the type of problems that should be solved on site, without reference to higher authorities, should be drawn up in the planning stage, so that each group knows what they can fix and what they need to escalate. It is impossible to draw up a definitive list for projects in general, but the guidelines in Table 10.1 may help:

Table 10.1

Type of problem	Impact	Who should handle it?
Local, easy to fix with available resource	Little impact in terms of time, cost, resource or quality	The local team. Keep a record
Local, easy to fix, needs more resource	Little impact on quality, has a cost in terms of resource	The local team, sign off from Local project manager, report to main project manager if necessary. Keep a record
Local, affects other teams or time scales	Small impact in terms of time, cost and other teams. No impact on quality	The local team will probably handle the problem, but the main project manager will need to inform and update any teams affected, and possibly sign off extra resource. Keep records
General, affects other teams or processes	Impact in terms of time, cost, other teams and quality	Main project manager must be informed and needs to handle impact on other teams and processes. Keep records
Local or general, affects the overall quality of the project	Quality impact	Main project manager must be informed. Keep records

10.3.2 You are their customer

This is the corollary of Section 10.3.1. They may be outside your direct control but you are their customer and presumably they wish to do business with you. Consequently you are, potentially, in a strong position to bring pressure to bear if they do not meet their obligations to your project. There is always a risk if the project is heavily dependent upon any one supplier and this should have been worked through at the negotiation with the supplier. This type of negotiation looks at the 'what ifs' of a contract:

- 'What if the supplier goes bust?'
- 'What if the supplier doesn't deliver on time?'
- 'What if the goods or services are not up to quality?
- 'What if the supplier can't get the raw materials?'

and so on. Penalty clauses in contracts are often used to cover these possibilities

Not only should the project manager have contingency plans for his project, but it is fair to expect the suppliers to have contingency plans for themselves.

10.3.3 Have own goals/objectives

Any third party will be operating to its own set of goals and objectives, some of which you may know but others you will not. Although you may not be able to establish what these goals and objectives are it is sensible to be aware that they may conflict with those of the project.

This can be a real problem with suppliers of materials, for instance concrete, paint, pipework, etc. You specify that these must be of the highest quality possible within the cost constraints of the project Your objective at this point is to purchase the best quality at a reasonable price. The supplier on the other hand has an objective to make the highest possible margin on what he supplies. Whereas you want to go to the highest common denominator, he will want to go to the lowest common denominator. This can be solved by carefully, and in detail, specifying exactly the quality of what you want.

10.3.4 Have own ways of working

This is often one of the most difficult things to cope with. Most people/organizations have their own ways of doing things which can seem strange to outsiders. It is very important when dealing with third parties that you stick to what they are supposed to be delivering rather than how they go about it. Provided they are delivering to budget, time-scale and quality then you have nothing to complain about.

There may be possible exceptions to this if the third party is causing the customer grief or adversely affecting the performance of the project team by their actions or if certain projects may require that the work is done under certain safety or legal constraints. This may not be the way that third party suppliers are used to working, so specification of necessary working practices at the time of contract negotiation will be necessary.

Suppose you are project manager of a project to install a large network of personal computers. This is a long-term project where you only intend to install a few machines per month over a period of two years. The supplier of the hardware prefers to produce his product in large batches, but you only need three per month, and have nowhere to store any extra machines. The hardware supplier points out that he can only supply in batches of a hundred. Instead of trying to make the hardware producer change his way of working, it would be better to organize storage for the finished machines.

10.3.5 Know things you don't

The fact that you are employing a third party implies that they have skills/knowledge that you don't. Consequently, it is vital that communications channels are established which allow the supplier to inform the project team of anything which can affect their ability to deliver what is required.

For example, you might employ a sub-contractor to get some promotional material printed. You might have the words and the illustrations already, but you would need their advice on subjects such as how many colour pages to use, what sort of paper is suitable, how to make best use of the paper in terms of layout and design. You don't know this and if you don't tap their expertise and just tell them to 'do what we say' you can end up paying much more than you should and not even end up with what you needed in the first place.

10.3.6 Don't know things you do

This is the other side to Section 10.3.4. The supplier may not know things that you do. This can be because you haven't communicated information to them, or because you have assumed that someone else has or believe that they will divine it for themselves!

For example, you may be employing a sub-contractor to install data and power cabling in premises where you are later going to install computer equipment. Your staff may have been to each site to survey them and have a record of any peculiarities such as there being a need to book a parking space two days prior to arrival to do work. If this has not been passed on to the supplier – perhaps the only information they have been sent is the wiring diagrams – then they will have problems when they turn up and there is nowhere to park their van. This may sound trivial but the time and cost impacts on the project may be substantial.

10.4 Communicating with third-party suppliers

One of the principal means available to the project manager to deal with the key points described above is to make sure that there are first rate channels of communication between the supplier and the project team. Not only should specifications and tasking be absolutely exact but it really helps if the project team take the time to get to know the third parties they will be working with. Reporting structures and contact information needs to be available, with possible back-up people listed in case the primary contact is not available. It is quite often easier to contact people within your own venue and organization than to contact external suppliers, so allow extra time in your contingency plan to cope with any possible delays.

10.4.1 Supplier meetings

The rules for running successful meetings mentioned in Chapter 9 apply to all supplier meetings, with the addition that it is important that all such meetings are minuted, so that a permanent record exists. It must be agreed by all concerned that the minutes document what actually occurred. This saves much grief should there be snags in the project, and penalties or blame need to be apportioned.

10.5 Summary

For any project external suppliers deserve careful scrutiny. They are beyond the direct control of the project manager or the project team and so can seriously impact the project if they fail to meet their obligations. External suppliers are not necessarily just separate organizations but may be from different groups within the same organization with different priorities to the project team. Communication with third party suppliers is therefore even more important than it is within the team itself. Failure to ensure that the supplier knows what is expected where and when is one of the most common causes of project hiccups and has the added pitfall of leading to animosity between people who should be on the same side. It is all too easy to forget the customer altogether whilst sniping at each other.

10.6 Exercises

10.6.1 Dealing with third parties

You are managing a project to develop a new stock control system and then train every stockroom worker in your company on the use of this system. Although the requirements and basic specification for this system have been defined by the logistics department within your company you will need to use four outside suppliers:

(a) a group of external computer software designers to produce the programme (StockData Inc.).
(b) an external computer manufacturer to make new screens and keyboards for your existing computers (Superkit UK Ltd).
(c) an external installation company to install the new screens and keyboards and check that they are working (InstallAll & Co.).
(d) an external training organization to implement the training (AXD Training Solutions).

Draw up an organization chart showing who will report to who, with dotted lines showing where there may be a need for the external suppliers to communicate with each other.

If it can go wrong, sooner or later, it will. Murphy's First Law

11.1 Introduction

Real life never goes according to plan so it is inevitable during most projects that things will go wrong. This chapter covers what to do when this happens. The emphasis is not on the revision of plans and contingencies, etc., but the personal and organizational skills that are needed to deal with unexpected changes, personal conflicts and time scale problems.

11.2 What went wrong?

What went wrong usually falls into one of these main categories:

- Unexpected factors – these come to light during the progress of the project and affect the project plan seriously.
- Conflicts – these may be within the team, between the team and the customer, the team and suppliers, or external conflicts that impact on the team's ability to deliver the project as planned.

11.3 Change control

Failure to have a proper change management or control process in place is a potential source of disaster in any project. Almost all projects are destined to find their goals and requirements subject to change at one time or another. These changes may be relatively trivial in nature affecting only the detail of the project. However, they can also be fundamental.

For example our latest project to build a conservatory between the side of our house and our garage, and to re-roof the garage with slates went along fine until we discovered, when we removed the roof of the garage, that the load bearing wall was not strong enough to bear the weight of the new slates. This meant a replan in terms of time, cost and design. Fortunately the builder immediately informed us of what he had found and together we replanned. Because there was complete openness between us and we had a contingency plan, the impact on the project, although severe was not painful. However, in another case, where we needed a new communication system installed, we found all sorts of unexpected problems, not least being the inability to contact anyone on the installation team who could help us, and being given imprecise and at times wrong time scales. The amount of stress and effort caused by this made the whole project not only late, but an unpleasant experience.

Failure to take proper account of the changes and to communicate them effectively to the project team will lead to situations where various members of the team are working towards conflicting goals. Once this has occurred not only does the team function less efficiently but the conflicts can have a disproportionate effect compared to their cause.

A description of change control is given in Chapter 6 of this book. In summary the key points are having a means of recording requests for change, assessing the impact of these changes on the project and either accepting or rejecting them prior to revising the project plan.

11.4 Conflicts between people

Inevitably there will be times in the life of a project when personal conflicts arise. These may be within the team or with suppliers or customers.

11.4.1 Causes

What causes conflict? Practical research has shown that there are several major factors:

- Assumptions – These are unspoken beliefs held by yourself or others that colour the way you look at the world. These unspoken beliefs may not always be true.
- Communication failure – When communication is poor you can be working with incomplete or inaccurate information.
- Priority – Where individuals have different priorities.
- Speed – Where people have different speeds of working.
- Status/territory – This concerns space, money, power and ownership, whether of things, places or ideas.

The following mini-case studies expand on these causes:

1 Assumptions

Philip, the project manager, knows that the time scales for the design he has been working on with Mary have been changed. Instead of three days, they now only have 24 hours. The following conflict arose:

Philip (who has assumed that Mary has been told about the change): 'We need that secondary specification now.'

Mary (who is working on the old schedule and thinks she has three days left): 'You can have it tomorrow morning.'

Philip (who thinks that Mary is being obstructive): 'No, I must have it now, or it puts everything back.'

Mary (who thinks Philip is hassling her unnecessarily): 'Get off my back, I've done everything to time so far.'

Philip (who is more aware of the time pressure and so more stressed): 'But I must have it now...'

What could Philip have done to avoid this conflict?

It is dangerous to assume that everyone's knowledge base is the same, or indeed that everyone's priorities, likes, dislikes and so on are the same as yours. If in any doubt, check.

2 Communication

Poor communication, laziness or imprecision in giving instructions and not checking that your message has been understood can lead to all sorts of problems. Here is an example of a simple misunderstanding plus the deadly assumption that occurred through careless communication and then concatenated.

It was 5.00 p.m. Janita, the project manager, needed a courier to collect a set of specifications from the main reception desk at her company headquarters and deliver it to the architect who was leading the project on site. It was vital that the parcel was delivered within the hour, or the project would be held up.

She asked her new secretary to ring a courier company and arrange this. The secretary tried their usual courier but couldn't get through so she rang another local firm which she had never used before and asked them to collect 'a parcel' from reception.

She then hastily parcelled up the specification, put its destination on the front, and sent it via a friend (who was going down to reception anyway) who took it to the rear security desk at the back of the company headquarters where couriers usually collected parcels. Because Janita's secretary was in a hurry she didn't add any information about the source of the parcel or who was supposed to collect it. She then left the building. The friend dropped the parcel off at the rear reception desk, and since there was a queue she didn't actually speak to the security guard on the desk.

The Speedy Courier arrived promptly, went to the front reception desk at the entrance to the company headquarters and asked for the parcel.

'What parcel? Parcels are collected from the rear desk.'
The courier went round to the rear desk to collect the parcel.
'What parcel?' said the security guard from behind a huge pile of parcels.
'I dunno,' said the courier, who was getting fed up with all the inefficiency.
'Can't help you then,' said the security guard. 'There's no one here now, they've all gone home, I'll sort it tomorrow.'

So, for the lack of simple information and clear communication the deadline was missed. The following day, Janita, in high dudgeon blamed the secretary, the secretary blamed the guard on reception, the guard blamed the courier and the courier company charged for the call. Finally the project was put back two days, because it took a day to find the original parcel.

What would you have done to not only make sure that this did not happen, but to also set a good pattern for the future?

3 Priority

The project manager is the only person involved with a project who has a complete overall view of the project itself and how it is going. The rest of the project team will be focusing on their particular tasks and responsibilities – usually things that they are good at, enjoy doing or place high value on. Certainly they will regard their priorities as important and will fight for extra resource, budget, extra time and extra attention.

Think of this scenario. The project (on a tight budget) is to redecorate and refurnish a house and to landscape the garden within a month. The interior designer wants to use the finest materials, the decorator thinks that the silk wallpaper that the designer has chosen will cost twice as much as ordinary wallpaper to hang and will take twice as long, the curtain maker wants to change all the existing curtain rails and the landscape gardener wants to plant mature shrubs and trees so that the garden will look good straight away. There is not enough money for all these things.

The project manager is in the middle. All the sub-contractors are keen to do the best job possible, and unless the project manager can arbitrate and decide the real priorities, squabbling will ensue with each person, quite naturally, pushing as hard as possible for their own point of view.

Clear briefing, consultation involving all interested parties and tight budgetary control would solve this problem.

4 Speed

We all have different speeds of working. Some people are cautious, perfectionist, like to take their time and make no mistakes. Others are happy to rush into new challenges, getting things going quickly and losing interest when routine or mundane tasks need doing. Others are slow to start because they are uncomfortable without a careful briefing. Others become impatient if they have to wait. Whatever speed they work at, they are all doing their best and all have the same goals – to finish the project, on time, to the right quality and at the right cost. Taking an average time scale for all workers is not much use here. When planning, the project team should have looked at the real speeds at which real people do things before putting a hard timetable in place.

If you, as the manager of a project are the sort of person who likes to get on with things quickly, you may well be putting unnecessary speed pressure on slower team members who work at a different pace from yourself. As long as the schedules are met, it does not matter what actual speed people work at. By hurrying up and chivvying slower team members you may actually affect the very qualities of perfectionism and exactitude that make these people so useful. Equally, if you like to do things slowly and carefully, try not to muffle the enthusiasm of the faster team members. Your golden rule should be: If it gets done on time and to the required quality and budget then let the team get on with it at their own speed.

5 Status/territory

We are territorial animals. We defend our own patch fiercely and often feel uncomfortable when on other people's territory. In project working there is very often the need to work outside our own territory where not only might we feel less comfortable, but may unwittingly impinge on someone else's space. This does not only apply to physical space, it equally applies to status, ideas and people. The project manager needs to take this into account. If at all possible the project team should have a space where they feel that they as a team belong (a designated meeting room or project office for instance). It is also part of the project manager's job to ensure that the project team does not behave like an invading army – taking over other people's territory without so much as a by-your-leave. The project manager needs at times to act as a diplomat, smoothing the path not only for his team, but also for anyone who is affected by the project itself.

What conflicts have you experienced or observed in the last two weeks? What do you think was the cause of these conflicts? Do the causes map onto the generic causes given above?

11.5 Good conflict handling

With good management, possible conflicts can be identified before the event and steps taken to avoid them. Nonetheless conflict will arise, so a strategy for coping with it is necessary.

Here is a set of rules to follow the moment a conflict arises:

Don't ignore it - if you pretend it's not happening it will get worse.
Define the problem carefully:
  – What has gone wrong?
  – What caused this to happen?
  – How do the people involved feel about it?
● Look at both sides of the conflict.
● Make sure that each person involved in the conflict has stated their viewpoint:
  – No interrupting.
  – Find out what has actually occurred, not what they think should have happened.
  – Keep personalities out of it.

- Clarify unclear points.
- Be as precise as possible.
- Summarize at the end of each statement.
- Analyse the causes:
  - Without allowing interruptions.
  - Keeping to the subject.
  - Don't use 'blaming' language.
  - All sides to put their case.
  - Summarize.
- Look for a solution:
  - Each party to define what they would like as an outcome.
  - No interrupting.
  - Look for positive outcomes.
  - All solutions to be reasonable within existing limits and restrictions.
  - Be creative.
- Select a solution:
  - Believe that a solution is possible (it almost always is).
  - Work towards a solution that suits everyone.
  - Think of the consequences if the conflict is not resolved.
  - Be fair.
- Implement the solution:
  - Make an action plan.
  - Communicate throughout the resolution of the conflict.
  - Give feedback.
  - Put in controls (deadlines) for remedial action or procedures to ensure that changes happen.
  - No recriminations.
  - Be positive.
  - Have realistic time scales.
  - Keep a record of what is agreed.
  - Both sides need to agree.

11.5.1 Strategies for handling conflict

There are three possible strategies for handling any conflict. You can handle it aggressively, passively or assertively. The aggressive strategy either insists that one side wins and the other side loses or dismisses the opposition as being not worth considering. The passive strategies try to pretend that the conflict isn't happening by putting it off or coming to a compromise situation where no one is completely satisfied. The assertive strategies look at both sides of the conflict and finds the best solution possible.

1 Aggressive strategies

Use these with care. Aggressive, insensitive conflict handling always leads to a win/lose solution where someone is left with the feeling that they need to balance the scales in their favour next time. If you are in conflict with people who you need to work with in the future, or who have an on-going relationship that is vital to the rest of the project, be careful how you use these strategies. There may be times when you feel forced to use an aggressive 'I win/you lose' strategy (for instance over safety, quality or legal matters) but be cautious with this; a problem solving approach with clear ground rules is a better way of getting a resolution, where although the 'loser' knows he/she has lost, they do not feel cheated or done down.

2 Passive strategies

Ignoring or putting off conflicts is a dangerous pastime for a project manager. Problems do not generally go away and if you as a project leader have a 'peace at all costs' or 'don't bother me with problems' attitude, the project team will hide conflict and problems from you until they are so great that they can be ignored no longer. An example of this occurred during a project we know of where the project leader hated confrontation. He would do anything to keep the peace. Consequently the secondary teams in the project put up with late deliveries and sloppy order fulfilment from a particular supplier and tried to sort things out for themselves. What they had not realized was that many little snags has built up to a real shortfall that finally put the project back for several weeks. When the extent of the problem was clear the project manager demanded 'Why didn't you tell me sooner?' To which the only answer was 'You told us not to bother you with little problems.'

The passive strategies tend to end up with a lose/lose situation where no-one gets what they want.

The only time to put a conflict off is when tempers are so high that no one is making any sense; in this case there should be a defined cooling off period and *then* the conflict should be faced.

3 Assertive strategies

These are the win/win strategies where a true resolution of the conflict is the end result. An assertive approach is based on mutual respect for each side involved in the conflict. A positive attitude towards solving the problem exists throughout discussions and an open, fair atmosphere is encouraged. Following the conflict handling rules outlined in Section 11.5 will lead to assertive conflict management.

11.5.2 A final word on conflicts

Conflict is not impossible to handle if you keep a sense of proportion and act swiftly. Use your common sense, stick to the facts, don't put things off and act positively. Blaming, nagging or forcing people into untenable positions is counter productive – you will end up with resentment and hostility that may affect the smooth running of the rest of the project. It is very rare indeed in a business project that conflicts cannot be solved with good will on both sides.

11.6 Wise words

The quotation at the start of this chapter 'If anything can go wrong, sooner or later, it will' has been listed as Murphy's First Law. Just so you know that things that go wrong don't just happen to you and have almost always happened to someone else first, we've listed some derivatives of Murphy's First Law, and a few others to make you feel better.

- 'Nothing is ever as simple as it seems.'
- 'Everything takes longer than you expect.'
- 'Left to themselves things go from bad to worse.'
- 'If you play with something long enough you will certainly break it.'
- 'If everything seems to be going well, you have obviously overlooked something.'
- 'It is impossible to make something foolproof, fools are very ingenious.'
- 'Constants aren't, variables don't.'

In other words if you haven't had something go wrong in a project then you haven't managed one yet. Don't worry about it, deal with it.

11.7 Summary

Once you have established that something has gone wrong then following the project management process of define, plan and implement can be used to get things back on track again. In some ways coping with things going badly wrong is very much the same as coping with change. The principal difference is that things will seem to be rather urgent at the time. In addition the project manager needs to be aware that conflicts require the use of personal skills as well as planning skills.

11.8 Exercises

This was a real two-year project involving the restoration of a small chapel on a private estate in France. The tasks to be performed were as follows:

11.8.1 Case study

(a) The chapel needed re-roofing with new guttering and flashing.
(b) The floor needed to have the original tiles taken up carefully and to be re-floored with a concrete base and the original tiles carefully laid back in place.
(c) The walls had to be stripped of the old plaster, sealed, re-plastered and then new plaster carvings put in place.
(d) The altar needed to be taken out, restored and replaced, with new painted panels inserted.
(e) The chapel needed completely re-wiring with a lighting and a sound system put in place.
(f) The re-plastered chapel needed painting and the plaster mouldings needed gilding.
(g) A new stained glass window needed to be made and installed.

The people involved were as follows:

1 The builder, responsible for the roof, floor and re-plastering. He worked thoroughly and the tasks he needed to do did not require particular artistic skill.
2 The plaster carver. A painstaking worker who took his time.
3 The altar restorer. An artist who couldn't and wouldn't hurry.
4 The artist (altar panels) who was temperamental but excellent and wouldn't guarantee a delivery date under a year.
5 The electrician, fast and efficient.
6 The stained glass window maker, quick and efficient although the process takes a long time.
7 The painter who always worked to time and quickly.
8 The gilder who worked slowly.

How would you organize the work? What was dependent on what? Where do you think the hold-ups might be and what could you do about this?

It is what you learn after you know it all that counts. John Wooden
It's not over until the Fat Lady sings. Music hall saying (attrib. various)

12.1 Introduction

This final short chapter covers the elements of a successful ending to a project: customer acceptance, handover and succession and project debrief.

As mentioned in Chapter 2, once a project is over it is very valuable to have a debrief session. At this time it is also necessary to make sure that all the t's are crossed and the i's dotted.

A project to organize a the staging of a sales conference might be seen to finish when the conference is over and the last delegate has left. But is this really the end? There will be outstanding issues like checking and paying the bills, doing a delegate satisfaction survey, checking with the speakers that everything was to their satisfaction, checking that all the equipment has been returned to store and that it is in good condition and a host of other small tasks that must be completed before the project can be truly put to bed. In the euphoria of having done well (or indeed the gloom of not having done as well as you hoped) it is very easy to let these final tasks slip. Time should have been allocated in the project plan to cover these. This wind up should take place as soon as possible after the project is over and while facts are still fresh in everyone's mind.

Apart from the important factor of customer satisfaction, there are other outcomes from a project. There may be the possibility of future business from the same customer. The project itself may have created new, and better working practices. Methodologies may have been developed during a project that could be used in other parts of the business. Suppliers may have been identified as excellent (use them again) or dreadful (don't touch them with a bargepole). Problems may have been identified that need fixing before other projects are undertaken. Project team members may have been identified as having unexpected skills which can be used in future projects.

All this information is useful to your business, and failure to collect it and act on it wastes future opportunities.

12.2 Customer acceptance

The beginning of the end of a project is customer acceptance. Until this has taken place the project cannot really be said to be complete. Of course, what signifies acceptance varies considerably from project to project. In some cases it is simply the fact that the bill has been paid. In others it is a highly formal procedure involving a vast array of signatures and forms and extensive testing schedules.

In essence such acceptance is defined by terms that were, or should have been, agreed before the project commenced.

12.2.1 Acceptance criteria

Typically such criteria fall into one of the following categories: performance; reliability; usability; quality.

1 Performance

Typically how fast, how economically, how frequently, etc. For example a computer system might have to guarantee to respond to the operator within a certain maximum time limit and store a given amount of information. An aeroplane might have to achieve take-off within a certain minimum distance for a given payload. These performance criteria will have to be tested, not only under test conditions but under normal working conditions. This may take several months where the project team itself is not actually involved in the testing, but may have to make adjustments as an outcome of these test results.

2 Reliability

Like performance this is a quantitative measure; it boils down to how often the project deliverables are allowed to breakdown when in normal use. The reliability of a computer system could be defined as the system being able to provide the service for 99 per cent of the time in normal working hours.

3 Usability

This is a 'softer' criterion. It can be related to the ergonomics of the end product, or the documentation or training materials that support the users of the end product.

Along with usability might go training. There may be a requirement for the implementer of the project to ensure that the customer's staff are adequately trained in the use of the deliverables. Indeed it may be necessary to provide 'train the trainer' deliverables where some customer staff are trained to train others in the future.

4 Quality

This will refer to the quality procedures that should have been followed whilst executing the project. Typically these are evidenced by documentation of procedures and completed activities that occurred during the project's life. Normally there would be an agreed quality system that was to be followed from the project start. These might be formal systems for design of software systems such as SSADM.

Consider the following projects: production of a new computerized payroll system, an extension to a retail shop, an automatic greenhouse watering system. For all these projects discuss what criteria might be used to determine the acceptance of the project.

12.3 Handover and succession

When any project comes to an end it is necessary to pass on information and responsibilites to those who will support it/operate it, etc. Often the project team will be dispersed and the support for the project will be passed on to a different part of the organization. A specific time should be allocated for the handover process and costed into the project's budget. Never hurry this part of the project wind up. Although you may know that the project deliverables have been successfully completed and work well, the customer will only believe this when he/she sees the project deliverables actually working. For example, a project to install new kitchens throughout a large hotel chain may look complete when all the gleaming equipment is in place and tested, but if the chefs and kitchen staff don't know how to use it the project is not yet complete. Even if it is not part of the project brief to train people in the use of the new equipment, you still have to hand on the knowledge of how to use it to someone who will do the training.

12.3.1 Project file

One of the benefits of finishing a project is that you can finally close off the project file. You no longer have to maintain it. However, it is important that it is included in the handover documentation and that it is available for future reference.

12.4 Project debrief

Before the final project party the well advised project manager will hold a project debrief meeting, or series of meetings to enable the lessons that can be learnt to be learnt. Typically these meetings, which may be with the team as a whole or with the individuals on-a-one to one basis, need to cover a range of topics.

The following checklist could be used for these meetings:

- What have we learned from this project in terms of personal, team and company performance?
- What have we learned about the client?
- Is it worth doing business with them again?
- Is there any future business possible from this project?
- Where were we seriously hampered by resource restraints and what should we do about this?
- What new ways of working, communicating, managing have we discovered from this project?
- What has been the overall impact of this project on our company?

The information gleaned from these meetings should be recorded and used as the basis for the debrief/final project report.

12.5 Summary

How a project is wound up is important. It is not enough to simply lock up the filing cabinet and leave a notice asking the last one out to turn off the office lights. The project manager is responsible for making sure that once the project is completed all the documentation is up to date, all the financial information is up to date and that handovers have been made to all those who are going to use/maintain/support the project deliverables after the event.

12.6 Exercises

12.6.1 Acceptance criteria

Why are acceptance criteria important?
Why is it preferable to get them agreed before the project starts?
List examples of such criteria for a manufacturing project of your choice.

12.6.2 Project handling

Why is it so necessary to have a project debriefing?
Prepare an agenda for a project debriefing session.

Sample answers

He who asks questions cannot avoid the answers. Cameroonian proverb

The very nature of project work means that there are often no 'right' or 'wrong' answers to specific situations. The answer is the usually just the best solution to the problem readily at hand. In other words a compromise. Consequently the questions asked in the chapters of this book do not have simple correct or incorrect answers. So, the sample answers here only outline the key points that you would expect to see from someone who had understood subject material. You may well find additional points to consider; if so don't worry, what matters is that you are thinking along the right lines. If you are unsure as to your answers then review the relevant chapters of the book and try again – better still, talk to someone else who has had to solve a similar problem in real life.

Chapter 2

2.7.1 What is a project?

Why isn't a production line manufacturing process considered to be a project whilst adding a series of identical conservatory kits to a series of different houses might be? Make up further examples from your own experience.

By definition a project is a one-off piece of work with a beginning and an end. A manufacturing process on a production line happens over and over again – it is a continuous process. Although each conservatory kit may be the same, each house/site will be different and different tasks will be required to install it in each case. In addition there will be different times that are convenient for the different houses so it will be necessary to schedule each installation accordingly – a project plan!

For your own examples, establish which have fixed start and end points and establish what their objectives are.

2.7.2 Why do they need managing?

List reasons why you think that projects cannot just be left to themselves. In small projects there may be no full time project manager – is the project still being managed?

Projects require that various discrete activities are performed in a particular sequence to produce the end result. This implies that some sort of plan must exist – however informally they are documented. For example: a corporal in the Army might detail his soldiers to get some rope and build a bridge over a rock chasm. This might all be communicated by word of mouth, etc., but there is still effectively a project and a plan. So, although there may be no full-time project manager, that does not mean that there is no-one planning the work. The key point is that projects don't just happen by themselves.

2.7.3 Life cycle

Although a project is defined in part by having a start and an end, the project life cycle has been represented as being circular. Why is it useful to look at a project this way rather than as a simple series of events leading to a conclusion?

The reality is that projects exist in a changing world. There are very many examples of this; e.g. by the time you have started work on a project the people who want it may well have changed their requirements. Similarly the environment in which the project team works will be changing, giving rise to different management constraints. Also, as the project progresses, people's knowledge increases and what may have seemed simple can become complex, or what seemed difficult become easy (though this is somewhat rarer!). As changes occur it becomes necessary to re-plan the project dynamically – consequently the process is an iterative one of defining, planning and implementing that starts at the beginning of the project and repeats itself until the eventual conclusion, hence the circular representation.

Definition

What are the main activities that need to be carried out in order to have completed the definition stage of a project? What information would you expect to have gathered during this stage?

The main activities are defining the project statement, the main objectives/goals and establishing the first level of planning detail including a work package breakdown structure, resource plan, basic risks, etc. See Chapter 3 for more detail.

Planning

Imagine that you have agreed to organize a concert for a friend who is just starting out on their solo career. List all the tasks that would need to be done and identify which you could do yourself and which you would have to put out to external suppliers.

You should be able to work this out for yourself. As a hint you would expect to book the room, decide the wording on the tickets, design the publicity yourself but you would expect to subcontract any printing and catering work that was required.

Implementing

Why are you likely to have to re-visit the definition and planning activities during the implementation of the project?

Simply because the world is a dynamic not a static place. As a minimum the passage of time will mean that what people think they want at the beginning of a project will have changed by the end of it. There are a number of reasons for this – one is that the project environment will have changed so that however well defined the original requirements were at the start they will need to be slightly (or even grossly) different by the end. Another is that by the very act of implementing a project the increased understanding that is gained tends to lead to a change in the perception of what is needed. This is analogous to the Heisenberg uncertainty principle in physics where you can know where a particle is or how fast it is moving but not both. The act of observation changes what you are looking at – so, by running a project you change what you eventually need.

2.7.4 Concerns

List the main causes of concern for a project. In each case give an example of how they can adversely affect a project.

Client; time-scales; budgets; communications channels; project teams; external factors; risk management. You should be able to make up examples from your own experience. However, here is a sample answer for time scales.

The project is to organize a banquet for 200 people in ten days' time. The caterers have told you that they need seven days notice of the menus – in particular they need to know how many need a vegetarian menu. This leaves you with only three days to find out the information required from 200 people. You have a time scale problem!

Chapter 3

3.12.1 Project definition

Imagine that you are the project manager for a project to design and build a prototype portable conference centre. Your team would include structural designers, consultants who know what customers would want from such a centre, architects, transport consultants, interior designers, electricians, plumbers, etc.
Produce a project statement for this project. How would you assess the validity of this statement?

The project statement must clearly cover the following: what the end result will be; what the time scales are; what the budget is. You should test your answer against these criteria.

A sample statement that meets these measures is:

'Design and build a prototype conference centre that must be no bigger than can be taken on a standard 10-ton lorry and be no more than 10 feet in height. The centre must provide seating for at least 20 adults and be capable of becoming operational on site within 3 hours of delivery to site. There must be basic catering facilities including the means of producing coffee and washing up cups, etc., as required. It must be capable of deployment in all normal UK weather and provide an acceptable environment for the conference attendees. It must come complete with the means of connecting to existing power, water, telephone and data services. The prototype must be available no later than six months after the project start date. The total budget for the project is £180,000 inclusive.'

3.12.2 Goals and objectives

Starting with the (or a) project statement identify as many goals/objectives for the project as you can. Use the SMART test to determine the validity of the goals and objectives. Revise these accordingly so that you end up with achievable ones. Do the revised goals fulfil the requirements of the project statement? If they do not what actions might you take?

Consider a project to move people into a house before they have to move out of their current lodgings. The project statement might be 'to move family A into their new home by a given date'. As described in Chapter 3 you should assess your goals/objectives to determine if they are Simple, Measurable, Achievable, Realistic and have a realistic Time-scale. Those that do not match up to this test should be revised accordingly. For example it may not be practical to decorate a complete house in a week, but it may be possible to decorate the kitchen, the bathroom and one bedroom perhaps allowing someone to move in early and avoid having to stay in an hotel. Where revised goals do not meet with the project statement you need to negotiate with the client to determine an acceptable alternative.

3.12.3 Deliverables

Define the deliverables for the portable conference centre. These deliverables should include both what is required to produce the prototype itself, what might be needed to support going from a prototype to a production unit and what might be needed to demonstrate the usefulness of the prototype to potential buyers.
Why is it important to agree deliverables with the client? Is it necessary for all the deliverables to be agreed with the client? Who else might you need to agree the deliverables with?

Examples of some of the deliverables might include: architectural drawings, technical specifications for building materials, specification of transport vehicles required, the prototype conference centre itself, engineering designs for a production line for production of the actual product, sales literature, promotional video of the prototype in use, site cabling/plumbing connection equipment, etc.

If you do not agree the deliverables with the project's customers (they may be internal to your own organization or outside it) then you have no means of demonstrating that you have completed it! You may have internal quality control deliverables for your own use and it may not be necessary to agree them with the customer, though it may well be in your interest to demonstrate that they have been produced to show an audit of the work you have done. You may also need to agree deliverables with other parts of your own organization, financial backers, quality control and personnel departments.

3.12.4 Work breakdown structures

Analyse the project for the portable conference centre and produce a WBS that takes into account the project deliverables and goals. Take this WBS down to the level where one box represents work that will only be carried out by one person. Why is it important to do this?

See example WBSs in Chapters 3, and 7.

3.12.5 Resources

For the WBS produced for Question 3.12.4 (or similar) identify the types of resource that would be required to deliver the project. Why can you only make an approximate estimate of the quantity of resource (staff and material) at this stage?

In the case of the portable conference centre you might have identified architects, mechanical engineers, electricians, plumbers, transport consultants, training consultants, interior designers, carpenters, labourers, etc.

It is difficult to identify exact quantities because you do not have enough information to identify exactly how many people might be involved in each activity to match up with time scale and/or budgetary constraints, etc.

3.12.6 Costing

Using the WBS that was produced for Question 3.12.4 (or similar) allocate the packages to the types of resource identified. Make up daily cost rates for these resources (or use real ones if you have them).

See example in Chapter 3. This gives you a sanity check on the scale and budget of the project.

3.12.7 Risks

Conduct a risk identification exercise for the prototype portable conference centre. Based on these risks do you consider the project would be worthwhile continuing with? How did you go about making this assessment?

Possible risks might include the inability of a 10-ton lorry to transport the finished prototype, not being able to meet health and safety/fire regulations for the prototype when in use as a conference centre, potential bankruptcy of sponsoring organization, failure of sub-contractors to meet the requirements for a promotional video in the time frame, etc.

As described you would assess the risks in terms of impact on the project and probability. At a guess the project is probably viable (portable offices already exist).

3.12.8 Project management discussion

Why is a project management discussion useful? If you are working in a group, carry out such a discussion for either a project you are involved in or the case study in these exercises.

Specifically it provides a forum for communication. The aim is to get together all the interested parties within your organization and make sure that they all know, and agree with, what is going to be done. The discussion should cover resources, technical issues, costs, legal and commercial factors, how the project will be handled, and the overall project viability. The benefit comes from reducing the chances of misunderstanding and maximizing the chances for the identification of risks, problems etc. It also provides an initial team forum for people to get to know one another.

3.12.9 The project file

What would you expect to have in a project file at the end of the definition stage of the project? What additional information might you plan to include at a later date as the project progresses? If you have completed the other exercises for this chapter, do you have the makings of a project file?

The project statement, identified goals and objectives, defined project deliverables, project file, risk register, cost estimate, work breakdown structure and a resource requirement. You would expect to both expand this and add to it as the project continues. See Chapters 4 and 6 for how it will evolve in detail. However, you would expect to have more detailed plans and estimates for cost, resource, time scales, reports, memos, minutes of meetings, specification documents, etc.

The answer to the last part of the question is yes! You do have the makings of a project file. You should be at the point where you are ready to move on from defining the project to planning and implementing it.

Chapter 4

4.12.1 Project planning

Produce a project plan for building a small business centre. This would require parking, office space, reception and meeting areas, computer and telephone facilities for up to 10 people. Use either a Gantt or PERT chart (see also Chapter 7). Although it is not necessary to cover all the aspects as you would for a real plan, do not over simplify. From the plan identify internal and external dependencies and what resources will be required when. Similarly identify any points on the plan which might make good milestones for either progress monitoring or triggering payment.

See examples in Chapter 4. Review your plan for practicality and logical sequence.

4.12.2 Resource

To what level must you break down the work to be done in a project? Why is this important?

Resource identification

You must break down the work to a level at which only one person is responsible for a´single activity/task.

This is essential if you are to eliminate the 'I thought he/she was doing/had done this already' type of problem. Also you cannot know if you have overloaded or over staffed a project unless you have a clear indication of what each person is to do.

Resource limitations

In the example given in Section 4.2.1, the 'build the walls' activity has been broken down to allow more than one bricklayer to work on it to reduce the overall time scale. Given that more bricklayers were made available to the project manager, what limitations might there be on further reductions to the time scale?

This is the old 'how many people can dig the same hole at the same time problem'. In some jobs there are physical limits as to how many people can work on it simultaneously, in other cases the administrative overhead from dealing with more and more people can overwhelm any increase in productivity from the additional staff.

4.12.3 Roles and responsibility

What factors would you consider when assigning roles and responsibilities to members of a project team? Why is it important that these are well defined and what measures would you take to ensure that everyone knew who does what?

The first step is to determine who has the right skills/experience to do the work. This must be extended to include personal skills as well as technical and professional ones, particularly where team leadership or dealing with third parties and customers directly is involved. It is important to ensure that the roles and responsibilities are defined to ensure that everyone knows precisely what they are supposed to be doing, when and who they need to deal with in order to get it done. Measures you might take to ensure that everyone knows who does what include personal and group briefing sessions and issuing organization charts – that are kept up to date – to all the project team, and third parties who need to know.

4.12.4 Dependencies

You have been made responsible to for the catering for a family birthday party at which there will be thirty people. Some are vegetarian, some meat eating. A room has been provided with kitchen facilities in which you can hold the party. The event is in a week's time and you have two people to help you who can shop, cook, set up tables or whatever will be required. You have to serve at least five courses of which three will need to be served hot. Produce a simple project plan for this that covers choosing the menu, determining what raw materials will need to be purchased, setting up the room, doing the preparation and cooking, serving the meal, etc. What internal and external dependencies exist within your plan?

See Chapter 4 if you are in any doubt as to what to do here. Typically you might find external dependencies on the raw materials supplier and internal ones on setting up the tables before the food can be put out.

4.12.5 Financial

Using the plan for the birthday party as a basis (or making up a new one if you prefer), imagine that you work for a catering company. You have been asked to manage the project and to produce a financial plan. You can assume that it will cost you £30 per person to provide the food and that the staff you use will cost you £5 per hour each and that you must use them in minimum quantities of half a day (4 hours) at a time. Your time costs £100 per day and your minimum charge out period is one day. You may assume that everything else is provided free of charge (FOC).

Calculate what the project will cost to deliver. What price would you charge if the company required you to make a 20 per cent margin? What price would you charge if you were required to operate a 20 per cent mark-up?

The client has negotiated an agreement where they pay for the party one month after it took place. Why might this reduce the overall profit of the job? How might you allow for this?

We leave you to do the sums yourself. With regard to the last question you might expect the profit to be reduced if you have to borrow money to pay for staff wages, materials (i.e. food), etc., before you are paid by the client. You could allow for this by incorporating the cost of borrowing into your overall price – i.e. treat it is an expense you incur up front; it is a real cost to you.

4.12.6 Risks

Consider a project to build an out-of-town shopping centre. Identify as many sources of risk to the project as possible. For all these risks make an assessment of both how likely they are to occur and how great an impact they might make on the project. Which of these risks would you consider when assessing the ongoing viability of the project? Why would you record all the risks identified not just some of them?

The answer for this is essentially the same as given for the risk question in Chapter 3 (Question 3.12.7). Just identify the risks then rank them according to severity and probability, etc. See Chapter 5 for more information on risks. The key point is that risk management never stops until the project is complete. You are reviewing the risks in the light of the greater knowledge of the project that you have gained since the definition stage.

4.12.7 Project file

At the end of the planning stage what additional information would you expect the project file to include? Who would you expect to have access to the project file, and would you expect there to be restrictions to access to the file?

The additions to the file should include: an agreed project plan (including Gantt/PERT charts, etc.); resource plan and organization chart; risk plan; revised and more detailed cost estimate; agreed time scales and deliverables; agreed change control procedures. It should also include all the outputs from the definition stage (revised if necessary), specifically: the project statement; identified goals and objectives; defined project deliverables; the risk register; an initial cost estimate; a work breakdown structure; the resource requirement.

You would expect the immediate project team, quality management and senior management for your own organization to have access to the file as needed. However, you would expect there to be restrictions relating to company/organization sensitive material, especially documents relating to cost and profitability information. You would not normally expect the customer to have access to the information in the file unless there was a special reason for this to happen. Access will be project/customer specific but you should aim to make everyone aware of as much as is going on as possible except where it compromises security or commercial confidence.

4.12.8 Opportunities

Why is it important to identify any non-project specific opportunities for the business or organization that is sponsoring the project? Either look at a project you are currently involved in or consider one which involves the design of a system for cataloguing video tapes. What opportunities can you identify? If there is no formal procedure for passing on such ideas within your organization, who would you inform?

This comes down to 'spin off' i.e. taking advantage of any benefits to your organization that come form doing the project work anyway. These benefits might be training related, a technical innovation, a new business opportunity, etc. But, if you don't look for them you won't find them.

4.12.9 Task scheduling

You are the project manager of a team who are to produce a new expenses processing system for a transport/courier company. The team will buy the computers, write the computer software, provide training to the operators and promote the use of the system within the company.

Perhaps 20 people are involved all together including technical programming staff, team leaders, trainers, buyers, personnel and accounting staff. How would you go about tasking these different staff? What information would you give to all of them and what would you make person specific? Where teams are involved, what involvement in this would you pass on to the team leader and how would you make sure that everyone involved was correctly tasked?

You must take the time to ensure that all team members are properly briefed. Section 4.8 gives the information that you need to pass on in general terms. Where you make the delineation between all staff and individuals will vary. However, the bottom line is that you restrict only information that applies solely to how one individual does their specific job. For example, you might tell all the decorators that the house was being painted but you might only tell the one painting the kitchen that it was yellow, particularly if that was the only room that would be using yellow paint.

Chapter 5

5.7.1 Risks

Consider a self-build housing project. Make a list of at least 20 things that you think might go wrong and then decide which of them can be planned for as risks, contingencies and dependencies.

Identification

Use the criteria given in Chapter 5, Section 5.3.3.

Assessment

For the risks that you have identified rank them according to both priority and probability. Which risks would you discard as being irrelevant?

You would expect to discard the low-impact risks though the high-probability ones might be treated as a contingency. You would take a case by case view on the medium- and high-impact, low-probability risks. You would make in-depth assessments on any high/medium impact, high-probability risks. You would, however, record all risks in a risk register in case they become more important later in the project – risk management is an on-going process.

Management

Why is risk management important? List some potential benefits of conducting a risk management exercise.

See Chapter 5 for detailed reasons, but the principle reasons are to avoid projects failing that shouldn't have been started in the first place, to allow action to be taken to minimize or eliminate risks, and to allow early detection of risks by identifying the warning signs that a risk is about to occur. The benefits are increasing the chances of delivering the project on time and to budget, minimizing the chances of wasting money and effort, minimizing the chances of total disaster.

5.7.2 Contingencies

What is the specific difference between a contingency and a risk? Why might some risks be converted to contingency plans during the life of a project?

Definition

The essential feature of a contingency is that it is something you have a plan for what you will do if and when it happens. You would normally make allowance for the cost of a contingency either as a sum of money you put by in case it happens or as an extra charge item to the customer. It is possible that as a risk becomes more probable that you might agree with a customer an action plan for dealing with it either at your or their expense (or on a shared basis); this is then essentially a contingency.

Example

For the house building project of Question 5.7.1 choose one of the identified contingencies and determine what actions you would take if it came to pass. How might you modify any cost estimates for the project accordingly?

The actions will be those activities that you have identified as being necessary to complete the relevant part of the project should the contingency occur. Modification to cost estimates you might make include: adding in the total cost of executing the contingency into the budget (worst case approach), making an estimate of how likely the contingency is to occur and taking a proportion of the cost accordingly, taking a view on all the contingencies for the project and assessing the overall impact on cost (some may be negative, some positive). Note that these cost considerations may or may not be passed on to the customer as a price consideration. The project manager does not always have control over price but should always know the costs that are to be incurred.

Plan

Consider that you are the manager of the project to implement the warehouse stock control system described in Section 5.4.1. You have been informed that there may be a requirement to use a different make of computer to complete the job because there could be a £5000 cost saving in so doing. The alternative computer is identical to that originally specified but has different power and data cabling requirements and is two feet taller. Make up a suitable, but simple, project plan and modify it to include a contingency plan that covers financial, resource, installation and testing areas of the plan.

An exercise for the reader!

5.7.3 External dependencies

Consider again the house building project of Question 5.7.1. For those items that you have defined as external dependencies which are the ones that you think are the highest risk and how might you plan ahead to cope with them? Would you treat them as risks or contingencies?

Again, an exercise for the reader; re-read the relevant parts of Chapter 5 if in doubt.

Chapter 6

6.8.1 Monitoring and control

Design a time sheet for a software development project. How might you ensure that the time sheet is completed on time?. What non-project specific elements would you account for?

One suggestion is to link payments to completed time sheets. Another is to offer a reward for consistent, timely, submission of the time sheets. You might consider including space on the sheet for holiday time, training (not paid for by the project/customer), non-project expenses, sick leave, etc.

6.8.2 Performing analysis

Consider a project for painting all the rooms in a large school building during the summer holiday period (i.e. when the building is not in use). Six painters are involved and the project should last five weeks. How might you assess the productivity of the painters? If the original plan assumed that one painter could paint one wall in two hours and you find that some painters do better than this, some worse, how might you forecast the actual completion date of the project after the end of the first week?

You might consider what area each painter covered during a day or a similar measure. When re-forecasting the end date you would look at how much work had been done and compare it with how many walls remained to be painted. If the walls are not of equal size you might assign the faster painters to the larger walls.

6.8.3 Report writing

Write a report detailing progress to date on a project you are familiar with – if you are not currently involved in one make one up or write one about your progress to date with your current training courses. Initially write this report for the 'project team', then re-write it for a customer and/or your immediate superior.
Write a financial status report for a project you are involved in, or make one up for a project to produce a prototype hedge-trimmer.

Review the report against the content of Chapter 6.

6.8.4 Project file

Why is it important to keep this file up to date? What are the potential problems that might arise from failing to do this? What strategies might you adopt to help keep the file up to date?

This file provides the central repository in which the state of the project, plans, costs, meeting minutes etc. are kept. If the information in this is out of date then anyone referring to it will be basing their actions on false information with potentially catastrophic results. The project file is part of the communication system of the project. Furthermore it provides part of the quality audit trail for the project providing a record of decisions made, etc. In addition you should consider the question of what would happen if the project manager were run over by a bus. If the project file is up to date then a new project manager would have a reasonable chance of taking over. The project file is an insurance policy. The problems arise from misunderstanding, the potential propagation of incorrect information – think of the potential impact of some members of the project team working to a different plan from the rest of the team. Strategies include making someone responsible for managing the file, regular audits of the contents of the file, etc.

6.8.5 Change control

You are the manager of a project to produce a prototype agricultural hedge trimmer. This device was originally specified to be operated by one person using a small petrol engine. As it is for agricultural use the device has been specified to be rugged, efficient and compliant with safety regulations but there has been no emphasis on quietness. The marketing department has decided that there is a domestic market for such a machine in the top-of-the-range electric powered machines. This would be mainly for those who had very large gardens with large hedges where it is impractical to use either a mains lead or a rechargeable system. However, to meet the needs of this market they have requested that you produce a version with an add-on extra silencer to make noise levels acceptable. Produce a simple project plan for producing the prototype and show how it might need to be changed to incorporate the new requirement. Produce sample change documentation in historical sequence that shows how you might go from change request to implementation. What factors would you consider when assessing the acceptability of the change? If you prefer a non-engineering example, consider a change request to a children's playground to give improved wheelchair access.

See Chapter 4 for example project plans, see Chapter 6 for example change documentation. When assessing the acceptability of a change you would consider cost, time-scale, resource issues and if the impact of these was justified by the benefits of making the change. It may be necessary to negotiate with the customer over the price that they are willing, or able, to pay for the change.

Chapter 7

7.11.1 General

Why are project management tools useful? What features would you expect to find in a project management tool? How might a computer/network based system offer additional benefits?

Largely because they make life easier by automating the drudgery and providing a common format for communicating information. See Chapter 7 for typical features. You might expect to benefit from a network based system because of the increased opportunities it offers for communicating project information amongst the team. This can be helpful for scheduling meetings, making sure everyone is aware of the latest state of the project, circulating change and risk information, etc.

7.11.2 Gantt

Make a Gantt chart for a project to move a small business from one office to another. What are the advantages of using Gantt charts?

Gantt charts are easy to understand, even for those unfamiliar with project planning. They are supported by most computer-based planning systems. It is easy to see what will happen when and who is responsible for it. With the computer-based tools it is simple to perform 'what if' re-planning exercises.

7.11.3 WBS

Using the plan from Question 7.9.2 as a starting point produce a multi-level plan for moving a manufacturing business from one site to another. The business employs about 200 people and has warehousing, engineering, transport and office facilities. These must all move during the same weekend and be operational by 09:00 on the Monday.

Check the plan to see if it works.

7.11.4 PERT

Production

Make a PERT chart for decorating a room. Identify the activities down to the level of the individuals who will perform each task.

Just do it.

PERT versus Gantt

Why might you choose to use a Gantt chart for this work instead of the PERT chart?

A Gantt chart is simpler to produce and understand than a PERT chart and is more suitable for small projects such as this one.

7.11.5 CPA

Identification

For the PERT chart that you have generated for Question 7.11.4 establish the critical path. Establish the minimum time that the job can be done. Why should you expect to revisit this analysis as the project progresses?

As the project progresses reality shows that tasks take different times to those originally estimated. Consequently what was critical on the original plan may not be critical once work has started, and similarly what was non-critical can often 'slip' and put itself on the critical path.

Benefits

What action might you take as a result of identifying the CPA? Why is CPA important?

You might dedicate extra resource to the critical tasks if this is appropriate, you might simply identify the tasks and give them a high visibility within in the project team, you might re-prioritize other tasks and use of equipment to give the critical tasks greater access to resources required to the complete them. This must be done with care as by over-concentrating on the critical activities, those activities that are not on the path can 'slip' and join it.

CPA is an important technique because it does allow the project team to concentrate on what is time critical and so increase the chances of delivery on schedule. However, it is worth noting that concentrating on the CPA does not mean that the costs of meeting the project are being adequately considered.

7.11.6 Project scheduling

For one of the project plans created for the exercises above, or a project you are involved in, schedule it to be completed in the minimum time. Now schedule it for the minimum use of resource. Making your own assumption for the hourly cost of the staff working on the project, estimate the difference in cost between the two schedules. Are there any other costs, e.g. overtime/shift working that might affect the costs? If so make an allowance for them. Are there any other problems that might affect the comparison?

Having looked at scheduling in the two extremes of time and resource limited, now define constraints for resource-limited scheduling such as no weekend working and no more than 5 hours overtime a week. Next try and schedule the project with the goal of getting the critical tasks completed as quickly as possible without breaking the resource constraints.

Produce the plans for yourself – compare with those in Chapter 7, etc.

Other problems that might affect the comparison include increased costs for delivering materials earlier (you might have to use an overnight courier instead of a regular delivery), you might need to buy the materials up front incurring cash flow and storage charges. Changing time scales affects more than just staff resource costs.

Chapter 8

8.5.1 Communication

Below is a list of the phases and their sub-stages in the project management cycle:

Definition phase

- *Project statement;*
- *Project objectives;*
- *Project management discussion;*
- *Work breakdown structure;*
- *Resource requirements;*
- *Risk assessment.*

Planning phase

- *Project planning;*
- *Problem analysis;*
- *Contingency and risk analysis;*
- *Contingency planning;*
- *Opportunity analysis;*
- *Resource manager scheduling.*

Implementation phase

- *Project monitoring and control;*
- *Project modification;*
- *Managing change;*
- *Performance analysis;*
- *Project end.*

By each phase and its sub-stages, note down the different types of communication needed for each. You will find that there is often the need for more than one type of communication during each phase and stage.
Types of communication:
a) Written (in the project file); b) Group meetings; c) Individual meetings (one on one);

d) Formal letter/report; e) Informal get together; f) Briefing document;
g) Formal presentation; h) Brainstorming session; i) On-site chat;
j) Motivational session; k) Memo; l) Up-date session.

As a starting point the following types of communication could be expected within the following phases:

Definition: a, b, c, d, f, g, h.
Planning: a, b, c, d, e, f, g, h, k, l.
Implementation: a, b, c, d, e, f, g, h, i, j, k, l.

However, you should be prepared to use any form of communication that will improve the chances of getting the job done on time and to budget!

8.5.2 Delegation

Why is delegation such an important skill for a project manager? Give at least three reasons.

- The project manager simply has not the time to complete all the tasks that a project needs.
- The project manager cannot be in two places at once.
- The project manager may not be as expert at some tasks as other people in his/her team.
- Members of a project team will not develop their skills unless they are allowed to take over and complete new tasks.
- People are motivated by having to learn and complete new tasks.
- Poor delegation skills can lead to faulty working practices and lowering of quality standards.

What should a project manager try to delegate and what should she/he never delegate?

Should delegate:
- Routine;
- Well defined tasks;
- Achievable by delegatee.

Should not delegate:
- Policy matters;
- Evaluation, discipline;
- Rewards, praise, etc.

8.5.3 Leadership

At the start of a project it is particularly important for the leader to do one particular thing. What is it?

Set clear SMART objectives and goals.

8.5.4 Negotiation

What are the five stages in a negotiation?

Plan, explore, offer, barter, close.

Chapter 9

9.5.1 Team formation

What are the three stages in team formation that need to take place before the team can perform well?

Form, storm, norm.

What happens during each stage?

- Forming – the team agrees its objectives and goals and knows as a team what is needed from them.
- Storming – the 'pecking order' and status issues within the team are defined.
- Norming – the unwritten behaviours that help the team to work comfortably together and give the team its identity develop.

9.5.2 Team roles

What are the four team roles needed for a healthy team?

Leaders, supporters, opponents and outsiders.

9.5.3 Groupthink

Why is groupthink so dangerous to successful teams?

The team becomes so self congratulatory and inward looking that they lose touch with the reality of the outside world and may cease to consider the viability of their project within the rest of the organization. Groupthink also leads to uncontested acceptance of decisions and therefore poor risk or opportunity analysis.

9.5.4 Meetings

List as many key points as you can that would lead to a successful meeting.

- Have an agenda;
- Make sure people know when and where it is;
- What they need to do before the meeting;
- Why they are invited;
- Record actions and decisions;
- Agree next steps;
- Keep it relevant.

Chapter 10

10.6.1 Dealing with third parties

You are managing a project to develop a new stock control system and then train every stock-room worker in your company on the use of this system. Although the requirements and basic specification for this system have been defined by the logistics department within your company you will need to use four outside suppliers:

(a) A group of external computer software designers to produce the programme (StockData Inc.).

(b) An external computer manufacturer to make new screens and keyboards for your existing computers (Superkit UK Ltd).

(c) An external installation company to install the new screens and keyboards and check that they are working (InstallAll & Co.).

(d) An external training organization to implement the training (AXD Training Solutions).

Draw up an organization chart showing who will report to who, with dotted lines showing where there may be a need for the external suppliers to communicate with each other.

A possible solution:

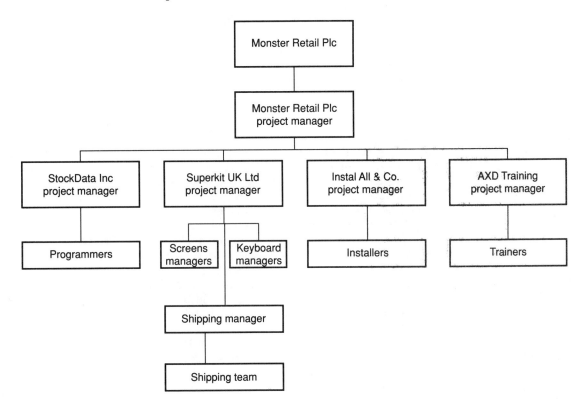

Chapter 11

11.8.1 Case study   *This was a real two-year project involving the restoration of a small chapel on a private estate in France. The tasks to be performed were as follows:*

(a) The chapel needed re-roofing with new guttering and flashing.
(b) The floor needed to have the original tiles taken up carefully and to be re-floored with a concrete base and the original tiles carefully laid back in place.
(c) The walls had to be stripped of the old plaster, sealed, re-plastered and then new plaster carvings put in place.
(d) The altar needed to be taken out, restored and replaced, with new painted panels inserted.
(e) The chapel needed completely re-wiring with a lighting and a sound system put in place.
(f) The re-plastered chapel needed painting and the plaster mouldings needed gilding.
(g) A new stained glass window needed to be made and installed.

The people involved were as follows:

1 The builder, responsible for the roof, floor and re-plastering. He worked thoroughly and the tasks he needed to do did not require particular artistic skill.
2 The plaster carver. A painstaking worker who took his time.
3 The altar restorer. An artist who couldn't and wouldn't hurry.
4 The artist (altar panels) who was temperamental but excellent and wouldn't guarantee a delivery date under a year.
5 The electrician, fast and efficient.

6 The stained glass window maker, quick and efficient although the process takes a long time.

7 The painter who always worked to time and quickly.

8 The gilder who worked slowly.

How would you organize the work? What was dependent on what? Where do you think the hold-ups might be and what could you do about this?

Work out what needs to be done on site and what could be done off site. This gives you a much larger time window for the work because a great deal can be done in parallel.

Work out the physical order in which tasks need to be done on site. Altar taken out, original floor tiles removed, roof and guttering repaired, walls stripped of plaster and resealed, floor concreted, new wiring for sound and light, re-plastering, painting, plaster mouldings added then gilded, altar replaced, floor tiles replaced, stained glass window installed.

The restorer, artist, plaster carver and stained glass window maker could then all do their work off site and, bearing in mind that the roof and general building work would take some considerable time, could do it within their preferred time scales.

The gilder, could work on site – which might cause a hold up, or it might be worth having the plaster carvings part gilded off site and then touched up when they were fixed to the newly plastered walls before final wall painting.

Chapter 12

12.6.1 Acceptance criteria

Why are acceptance criteria important?

The project cannot be said to be complete unless the customer is satisfied. The project team must know the acceptance criteria at the start of the project or the project objectives will not fulfil the measurable part of the SMART test.

Why is it preferable to get them agreed before the project starts?

So that there is no confusion about the quality standards and specifications of the project deliverables.

List examples of such criteria for a manufacturing project of your choice.

An exercise for the reader.

12.6.2 Project debriefing

Why is it so necessary to have a project debriefing?

To capitalize on any opportunities or threats for future business or projects which might have been identified during the project and to thank the team for their participation.

Prepare an agenda for a project debriefing session.

An exercise for the reader.

Glossary

Activity	Identified work to be done by person/team (see also Task).
Break-even	The point at which a project's costs equal the price charged for it.
Cash flow	Difference between moneys in and out within a fixed time period.
Contingency	An action/task that will be taken if a situation occurs.
Controlled document	A document which is subject to formal change control and which may also have a limited circulation which may have to be signed for.
CPA	Critical path analysis.
Critical activity/task	An activity which lies on the critical path for a project.
Critical path	A route map through all the time-critical activities/tasks between project start and project end.
Delegation	Effectively passing a task to another member of the team.
Deliverables	Anything that the project is required to produce in order to be completed.
Dependency	A requirement for an event or task to be completed before another one can start.
Float	Difference between time planned for a task and time available to do it.
FOC	Free of charge.
Gantt chart	Project planning chart.
Goals	Specific, measurable targets that a project is to meet.
Margin	The percentage of the price of the project that represents profit.
Mark-up	A percentage or fraction of the estimated cost of a project added to the cost to produce a price. (Margin is not the same as price!)
Milestone	A single measurable event in a project.
Objectives	What the project is expected to achieve within the business/organization that is sponsoring it.
Organization chart	A diagram showing who reports to who/who does what, etc.
PC	Personal computer.
PERT	Project evaluation and review tool.
PIM	Personal information manager.
Prime contractor	Organization with overall responsibility for delivering a project.
PRINCE	A project development system.
Project	Identified package of work with fixed start and end points.

Project file	Central collection of information that belongs to the project.
Risk	A threat to all, or part, of the project's viability/cost/time scale.
Risk register	A record of all identified project risks.
Spin off	Benefits derived from a project outside the original scope of the work.
Sub-contractor	Organization/person working for a prime contractor.
Task	Identified work to be done by person/team (see also activity).
Team working	Interactive way of working involving a group of people with common objectives.
Third party	Organization/person outside of the project team.
WBS	Work package breakdown structure.

Additional Reading

John Adair
Effective Time Management: How to save time and spend it wisely
Pan Books, London, 1988

Steven Beebe and John T Masterson
Communicating in Small Groups: Principles and practices
Harper Collins, USA, 1989

R. Meredith Belbin
Management Teams: Why they succeed or fail
Butterworth Heinemann, 1991

Derek Biddle and Robin Evenden
Human Aspects of Management
Institute of Personnel Management, London 1989

John Crawley
Constructive Conflict Management: Managing to make a difference
Nicholas Brealey Publishing Limited, London 1992

Gavin Kennedy, John Benson and John McMillan
Managing Negotiations: How to get a better deal
Hutchinson Business, 1989

The Industrial Society Handbook of Management Skills
Industrial Society Press, 1990

Trevor L.Young
How to be a better Project Manager
Kogan Page, The Industrial Society, 1996

Index

DUCHY COLLEGE LIBRARY